THE STORY OF ORDINARY PEOPLE LIVING IN EXTRAORDINARY TIMES

LOUISBOURG

EXPERIENCE THE HISTORY

SUSAN YOUNG DE BIAGI • PHOTOGRAPHY BY DAVID MACVICAR

FORMAC PUBLISHING COMPANY LIMITED

HALIFAX

Formac Publishing Company Limited thanks the Fortress of Louisbourg/Parks Canada for their contribution towards the French edition of this book. Formac Publishing Company Limited acknowledges the support of The Canada Council for the Arts for our publishing program. We recognize the support of the Nova Scotia Department of Tourism, Culture, and Heritage, and the financial support of the Government of Canada through the Canada Book Fund for our publishing activities.

Tourism, Culture and Heritage
Tourisme, Culture et Patrimoine

The Canada Council | Le Conseil des Arts
for the Arts | du Canada

Canada

The paintings "View from the Clock Tower" and "View from a Warship" by Lewis Parker reproduced by permission of the artist and Parks Canada (copyright held by Lewis Parker).

Canadian Cataloguing in Publication Data

Young de Biagi, Susan, 1957-

Louisbourg : experience the history / Susan Young de Biagi ; photography by David MacVicar. — New ed.

Previous ed. (1997) had subtitle: a living history colourguide.

ISBN 978-0-88780-905-7

1. Fortress of Louisbourg National Historic Site (N.S.) — Guidebooks. 2. Historic sites — Nova Scotia — Louisbourg. I. Title.

FC2314.L68B53 2010   971.6'955   C2010-902948-8

Formac Publishing Company Limited
5502 Atlantic Street
Halifax, Nova Scotia
B3H 1G4
www.formac.ca

Distributed in the US by:
Casemate Book Distributing
908 Darby Road, 2nd Floor
Havertown, PA 19083

Printed and bound in China.

CREDITS AND ACKNOWLEDGEMENTS

I would like to thank the following people, without whom this book could not have been written:

Bill O'Shea, Head of Historical Resources at the Fortress of Louisbourg, and historians Ken Donovan and John Johnston, for their valuable comments on the manuscript; Sandy Balcom, Curator of Furnishings at the Fortress of Louisbourg, for providing such generous access to the materials; Assistant Curator Brian Harpell for his vast knowledge of the collection and for always being on hand with an extension cord, a ladder or a helpful suggestion; Anne O'Neill of Visitor Services at the fortress, and her staff — Peter Chiasson, Sandra Larade and

Brad Postlethwaite — who worked miracles of scheduling and cheerfully tramped through the rain with us; my friend Heather Gillis, Archives Clerk at the fortress, for the long hours she spent tracking down maps and images; Judith Romard, Librarian, for the kind help and the peppermints; Eric Krause for valuable leads on sources; and Norman Munroe, photographer: it was a delight to watch you work. Thanks to Lynn Henry, editor at Formac, for her insight, patience and tact; and a special thank you to Mark Biagi for his perceptions, his comments, his sympathy and his car. Finally, thanks to B.A. Balcom, Sandy R. Anthony and Rebecca Duggan for proofreading.

CONTENTS

Louisbourg
A Map of the Fortress

1	Fortress walking tour
D	Open to the public
D	Military Demonstration
E	Exhibit
◻	Food service

C	Public Telephone
🚻	Public Washrooms
R	Rest area
62	Closed to the public
♿	Accessible Washrooms

1. Des Roches House
2. Dauphin Gate
3. Sentry Box
4. Spur Battery
5. Dauphin Demi-Bastion
6. Barracks
7. Powder Magazine
8. Postern
9. Quay
10. Lartigue House
11. Lime Kiln
12. Artillery Storehouse
13. Forge
14. King's Bakery
15. Armoury and Forge
16. Woodlot
17. Exhibit on military life (video)
18. Storehouse
19. Storehouse/Prison
20. Engineer's Property
21. Laundry and Stables
22. Children's Interpretive Centre
23. Merchant Storehouse
24. De Gannes House (Military Captain)
25. Ice House
26. Place d'armes
27. Guard House
28. King's Bastion
29. Chapel and Governor's Apartments
30. Soldiers' Barracks
31. Museum Exhibit
32. Ruins Walk
33. Parade Square
34. De la Plagne House
35. De la Vallière House
36., 37. De la Vallière Storehouses
38. Loppinot Ruins
39. Fizel Ruins

40. Dugas/de la Tour House
41. Exhibit in Carrerot House
42. Benoist House
43. L'Épée Royale
44. Hôtel de la Marine
45. Old Storehouse
46. King's Storehouse
47. Frederic Gate
48. Grandchamps Inn
49. Destouches Bakery and Gift Shop
50. Financial Administrator's Property
51. Stables
52. Dovecote
53. Carcan
54. LaGrange House
55. Beausejour Tavern (games and pastimes)
56. Delort House
57. Morin Storehouse
58. Cassagnolles-Detcheverry House
59. Santier House
60. Chevalier House
61. Baron House
62. Pièce de la Grave Guardhouse and Battery
63. Delort I Storehouse
64. Baron Storehouse
65. Delort II Storehouse

Louisbourg Harbour

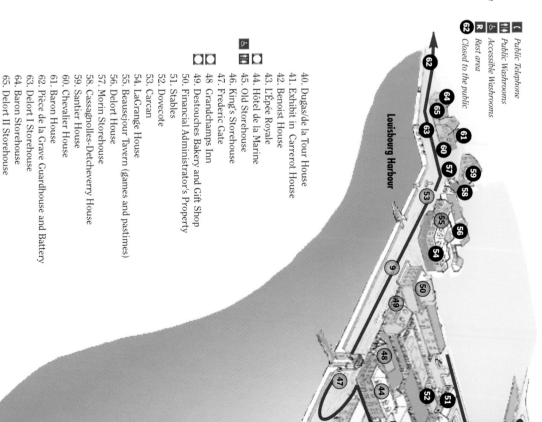

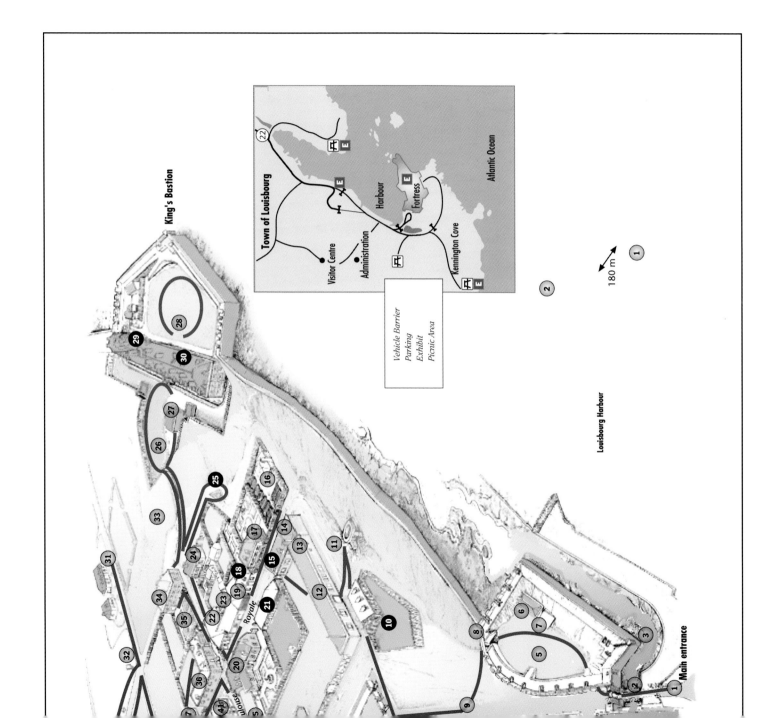

Town of Louisbourg

Visitor Centre

Administration

Harbour

Fortress

Kennington Cove

Atlantic Ocean

King's Bastion

Louisbourg Harbour

Main entrance

Royale

180 m

Vehicle Barrier
Parking
Exhibit
Picnic Area

PREFACE

The shallop remains an enduring symbol of Louisbourg's inshore fishery.

I first came to Louisbourg as a little girl of five. As I stood on the beach with my mother, she told me about the ships that twice came to capture the great fortress. With a child's fluid understanding of time, I believed those ships could return at any moment and strained to see them over the horizon.

In the 18th century, Louisbourg was the first landfall for ships sailing from France. For the passengers on those ships, it offered sanctuary from long days and nights on the cold North Atlantic. Once settled, the new inhabitants had no wish to leave this bright, busy port. The ocean became their link to the outside world. Each spring, as the ice drifted away from the coastline, the townspeople looked forward to the end of their winter isolation. Incoming ships carried news of family in France and brought French wine, cheese and other luxuries to starved palates. Twice, they brought invading armies.

The fortress was taken for the first time in 1745 and its settlers deported. When peace was restored, they returned from exile to rebuild homes blackened with cannon fire. The second time, there was no such reprieve. In 1760, the fortress was blown to pieces as its settlers grieved. Here in Cape Breton, we who cling with such tenacity to our island can understand their loss. So must anyone who strives to build a secure future in an uncertain world.

For many years, Louisbourg lay hidden under a thick cover of meadow grass. The barest outlines of stone traced the location of roads and buildings. With my young mind, I peopled the parade ground with soldiers and filled the empty gardens with vegetables. Later, in the 1960s, the dream became reality, as archaeologists, historians and artisans laboured to bring the ruined fortress to life.

Louisbourg's tragedy is that the hopes and dreams of a founding people were so quickly and brutally extinguished. Its triumph is that it has been rebuilt. Today's children can stand watch with the soldiers, play cat's cradle with a servant and dance to the folk songs of France. Each year, thousands of visitors watch eagerly for their first glimpse of Louisbourg's skyline. What do we seek, we who come to this small corner of the world? Perhaps some of us reflect on the forces that shaped this continent as France and England battled for supremacy. Perhaps, too, we remember the ordinary people who were lost in the nation's quest for empire.

It's still a habit of mine to scan Louisbourg's waters, looking for a sail. During a recent visit of international tall ships, I held my small daughter's hand as we watched the parade of sail move gently towards us. My own connection with Louisbourg had come full circle. And, after two hundred years, the ships had come back.

Susan Young de Biagi

FORTRESS LOUISBOURG ASSOCIATION

The Fortress Louisbourg Association was formed in 1976 to promote the study and appreciation of the history of 18th-century Louisbourg. Our objectives include participating, whenever possible, in the activities of the Fortress of Louisbourg National Historic Site, especially in civilian and military animation, extension programs, training, archaeology and research.

Our main activity is our very popular Children's Animation and Apprenticeship program. Each summer, children between the ages of five and 16 are brought on site, outfitted in period costume, and provided with a one-week educational 18th-century learning experience. The children are supervised and trained by our qualified staff, and the program is provided to children at a minimal cost. The program involves over 200 children annually, and there is a waiting list of more than 200 as well. The presence of the children on site adds greatly to the animation experience of every visitor to the fortress.

We also have many adult volunteers, including a Volunteer Militia, who give freely of their time to enhance the activities of the park. Since we have no ongoing source of revenue, we operate three period restaurants, two interpretive gift shops, a chocolate salon and a military bakery in order to raise funds for our various endeavours. These business operations result in the creation of 90 to 100 seasonal jobs and play a significant role in the economic development of Louisbourg and the surrounding communities.

For further information or to participate in the association, contact:
Fortress Louisbourg Association/Association de la Forteresse Louisbourg
265 Park Service Road
Louisbourg, Nova Scotia
B1C 2L2 Canada
(902) 733-2960
flaspecialevents@live.com

The fifer's elaborate uniform sets him apart from the ordinary soldiers who served in the Compagnies Franches de la Marine.

The story of Louisbourg is one of ordinary people living in extraordinary times. It tells of war uprooting the French settlers of Newfoundland, and sweeping them onto the shores of Ile Royale (Cape Breton), where they built the fortress of Louisbourg. Twice more, war would drive the settlers from their homes and fishing properties. In the end, Louisbourg's French settlers did not establish a future for themselves in the New World, but their struggle has become a part of North America's history.

The story begins in Newfoundland. By the 17th century, all of Catholic Europe was calling for fish. Each spring, fleets of European vessels stationed themselves on the Grand Banks off Newfoundland. In this "green" fishery, the cod was simply packed in layers of salt and carried back to Europe in time for Lent.

The settlers of Placentia in Newfoundland dealt primarily in the "dry" inshore fishery rather than the "green" offshore industry. Every day, small Newfoundland shallops deposited their catch on the shore. The fish were split up the backbone, salted, and dried on wooden stands known as "flakes." Because the dried, white product kept well in hot climates, it was highly valued in Spain, Portugal, and southern France.

Placentia's fishing proprietors were building prosperous businesses before war with Britain intervened in the early 1700s. When the hostilities ceased, they found that their livelihood had been signed away: in the 1713 Treaty of Utrecht, France gave up all her property in Acadia and southern Newfoundland and retained only two small islands—Ile Royale (Cape Breton) and Ile St. Jean (Prince Edward Island).

Ile Royale, in particular, was valued for its inshore and offshore fishing grounds—the same type of fishery the settlers of Placentia had engaged in so successfully. Indeed, throughout Ile Royale's history, the value of the island's fisheries consistently exceeded that of the Canadian fur trade. In September 1713, 149 settlers arrived at Ile Royale aboard the king's ship *Semslack*. These French fishing proprietors staked out properties all along the eastern and northern coasts and settled down to build new lives.

Louisbourg was Ile Royale's trading centre, and became its official capital in 1720; Ile St. Jean also fell under its authority. Soldiers from the former Placentia and from Quebec were sent to guard the new colony. In addition to protecting France's fishing interests in the area, Louisbourg served as an advance base for the French colonies along the St. Lawrence River. Enemy fleets that tried to sail up the St. Lawrence to Quebec would have to contend with Louisbourg first.

When war broke out again in 1744, Louisbourg took the offensive and attacked the British fishing settlement

of Canso, just 100 km (62 miles) down the coast on mainland Nova Scotia. Later that summer, Louisbourg forces besieged Nova Scotia's capital, Annapolis Royal (formerly Port Royal). The siege was lifted, however, when promised reinforcements failed to arrive from France.

These attacks alarmed the people of nearby Massachusetts, as did the presence of French privateers in their waters. When Britain showed no interest in launching a counterattack, Governor Shirley of Massachusetts appealed to his colony's General Court. Its members—prosperous merchants for the most part—were not averse to eliminating a competitor in the east coast fisheries. With Louisbourg gone, New England fishing fleets could command the entire eastern seaboard. In 1745, the neighbouring colonies of New Hampshire, Connecticut, Rhode Island, New York, Pennsylvania, and New Jersey all offered men and arms, or supplies. Commodore Peter Warren of the Royal Navy was ordered to provide naval support. On April 30, 1745, New England's land forces, led by merchant William Pepperrell and composed largely of volunteers and local militia, attacked Louisbourg. Thus began a siege that has been called the "Campaign of Amateurs" because of the inexperience of the attacking forces.

The artillery that defended Louisbourg was trained on the harbour. The Royal Battery (the ruins of which you may visit today) faced the mouth of the harbour. Another fortification, known as the Island Battery (also in ruins), was constructed on a small island at the mouth of the harbour. In theory, any ship that made it past the cannon

A member of the Swiss Karrer regiment stands guard far from his native land.

Long years of drill were not, in the end, enough to save Louisbourg from destruction.

of the Island Battery would be bombarded by the guns of the Royal Battery and town.

The New Englanders, however, did not attempt to force their way into the harbour. Instead, they landed in Gabarus Bay and attacked overland, emerging from the woods just behind the Royal Battery. The French, realizing the impossibility of defending the Battery from that vantage point, abandoned the fortification. Unfortunately, they chose to spike, rather than blow up, the cannons. The New Englanders promptly repaired the guns and turned them on the town. By the end of the siege, the New Englanders had also disabled the Island Battery. Once Louisbourg's main defenses were taken, the French command had little choice but to surrender. The garrison and civilian population were shipped back to France.

New England soldiers were left to guard the fortress over the winter. Lacking both clothing and firewood, 1200 men sickened and died of dysentery and infections brought on by the intense cold. The only satisfaction left to the survivors was the knowledge that they had eliminated a dangerous enemy. Yet even this was short-lived: the fortress

was returned to France in October 1748, by the Treaty of Aix-la-Chapelle. For twenty years, the New Englanders resented this cavalier surrender of such a hard-won prize.

The townspeople of Louisbourg were happy to see their homes again. By 1758, there were 3500 soldiers stationed in the town and the civil administration sought ways to develop the economy of the island. They opened a coal-mine in the area and, prior to the Acadian Deportation of 1755, encouraged Acadian farmers to relocate to Ile Royale, with limited success.

In the end, all the planning and hard work came to nothing. Britain and France were soon at war again. By June 1758, another enemy force was bearing down on Louisbourg and this time, it was 27,000 strong. The 13,000 attacking soldiers, mostly British regulars, were commanded by General Jeffrey Amherst. The British fleet, under the command of Admiral Edward Edward Boscawen, sailed from Halifax, Britain's newest naval base. Its 23 men-of-war and 16 smaller vessels were crewed by over 14,000 sailors. During the weeks that followed, the British command successfully repeated the strategy used in 1745.

By July 26, the fortress had surrendered. One of the leaders in the campaign was Brigadier James Wolfe, who would lead a British attack on Quebec the following year. For the second and last time, Louisbourg's settlers were shipped to France. To ensure that Louisbourg would never again be used against Britain, miners blew up the fortifications. This task was carried out under the supervision of the Hon. John Byron, grandfather of the British poet Lord Byron.

It would take another 200 years for Louisbourg's walls to rise again. The fortress was erected by the Government of Canada in the 1960s to commemorate the role that Louisbourg played in the history of North America. Today, the Fortress of Louisbourg National Historic Site covers approximately 6,700 hectares (16,550 acres) and is one of the largest historical sites reconstructed from the ground up. Furnishings from Europe and North America help recreate life in an 18th-century fishing and trading town.

VISITOR RECEPTION CENTRE

Your visit to the fortress begins at the Visitor Reception Centre, approximately 1.5 km (1 mile) beyond the modern town of Louisbourg. Admission includes the bus ride to the site, entrance to the buildings, and participation in guided walking tours. Full services are available between June 1 and September 30. During the month of May and from October 16 to October 31, guided walking tours of the park and of selected buildings are available at specified times. From November to April, private walking tours must be scheduled in advance.

After purchasing a ticket, most people take a few moments to view the interpretive exhibits in the Visitor Reception Centre. Film, books and other items can be purchased at the gift shop operated by the Fortress Louisbourg Association. The bus then carries all visitors to the fishing property, situated just outside the fortress walls. (People with special needs can make special arrangements with the receptionist at the Visitor Reception Centre to take their cars on site.)

To enjoy the experience to the fullest, visitors should plan to spend a full day on site. Joining in a guided walking tour takes an hour and a half, while exploring the buildings and chatting to costumed staff takes approximately four hours. Visitors also enjoy browsing among the ruins and sampling the food in the period restaurants.

The site's three restaurants, known as the Hôtel de la Marine, À L'Épée Royale, and the Grandchamps Inn, serve everything from full-course meals to light lunches. The Destouches Coffee Shop offers a choice of 18th-century pastries along with modern snacks and drinks, while the King's Bakery sells soldier's bread made from stone-ground whole wheat and rye flours.

Comfortable, modern seating areas are available in the Duhaget House, the de la Plagne House, and the residence of the *commissaire-ordonnateur*, and on the lower floor of the King's Bastion Barracks. Check the map for the location of washrooms.

During the summer months, temperatures at Louisbourg fluctuate widely between 12 and 23 degrees Celsius (50 and 72 degrees Fahrenheit). Even on a brilliantly sunny day, sudden fogs can sweep in off the sea, so take a thick sweater or jacket, preferably waterproof. Remember to wear a pair of comfortable shoes—18th-century roads can be rough and uneven.

As you walk from the fishing property to the Dauphin Gate, expect to be challenged by the soldiers. The interpretive focus is the summer of 1744, when war was raging in Europe and New England privateers were a scourge on Louisbourg shipping. The soldiers are understandably nervous and on the look-out for spies. Your trip into the 18th century is ready to begin.

The king's men on patrol

THE FAUXBOURG

The fishing proprietor's house is situated in the area known as the Fauxbourg, just outside the walls of Louisbourg. It is interpreted as the house of Jeanne Galbarette and her husband Georges Desroches. Their property was just one of many that encircled the harbour. Each fishing property had its own wharf, fish flakes, and huts for the workers. Shallops, the small boats of the inshore fishery, lay on the shore in various stages of construction. The smell of drying fish was on the wind. Since 1744, the sea level has risen almost a metre, obscuring any traces of the original houses along this shoreline. As a result, the fishing proprietor's house is the only reconstructed building in Louisbourg that is not built on an 18th-century foundation.

This property originally belonged to Jeanne's first husband, Joannis Dastarit. When they arrived in Louisbourg in 1717, the couple's first concern would have been to construct a shelter and set up the operation as quickly as possible. Many early colonists opted for the *piquet* (vertical log) construction, in which trees were simply stripped of their branches and set in a trench in the ground. The poles were then chinked with mortar to keep out the cold winds and blowing snow. Sod roofs were simple and effective insulators. Other settlers chose roughly hewn boards for the roof.

These humble fishing properties formed an important part of Louisbourg's economy. By the 1730s, resident fishermen accounted for approximately 75 percent of all cod landed on Ile Royale. In return for their contribution, they received the full protection of the law: only resident fishing proprietors could hire migrant workers or rent out beachfront property. With luck and shrewd management, some proprietors were able to move into the merchant class. They supplied other residents with fishing gear and goods on credit, in return for a share of the catch. By purchasing a schooner, a merchant could collect cod from outposts all around Ile Royale.

Others were not so fortunate. A bad season left many proprietors at the mercy of their creditors. Joannis Dastarit was one of those forced to declare bankruptcy. He had better luck as a tavern-keeper, serving food and alcohol to the Basque fishermen who arrived each spring. For these fishermen, the whole of North America was just a summer fishing camp. They spent their days on the cold and foggy sea around Ile Royale; at night, they took comfort in a bowl of hot soup in a tavern and a glass or two of West Indian rum, drunk around the fire. As Basques, they were isolated by language and culture from the French fishermen around them; however, as Jeanne and Joannis Dastarit were themselves Basques, from the area around Bayonne, their tavern was probably a centre of Basque life in Louisbourg. Jeanne ran her husband's business after his death—and ran it well. By 1728, she had acquired two properties in town. Her second husband died after only one year. She had more luck with her third husband, Georges Desroches. The pair wed in 1738, when Jeanne was 69 years old and Georges was 28. Theirs was a long and successful partnership. Jeanne ran the tavern, while Georges Desroches built up the fisheries end of the business. Before long, Georges Desroches was the owner of a 40-ton ship, the *St-Pierre*, and several shallops.

The first siege left this fine property black and smoking. Still, the Desroches' did not leave Ile Royale during the English occupation. Jeanne's age, 76, may have been a factor. When the French returned, the couple rebuilt their property outside the town walls. Jeanne Desroches did not live to see Louisbourg's second siege. She died in 1754, leaving the business to Georges. As his name did not appear on the list of Louisbourg residents who arrived back in La Rochelle, France, in 1759, his fate remains unknown.

Opposite page (top): Storage hut, with piquet construction

Opposite page (bottom): Humble fishing properties formed the backbone of Louisbourg's economy.

Top: A hearty Basque soup

Bottom: The Desroches tavern was a haven of warmth and comfort in an uncertain climate.

In wartime, soldiers at the Dauphin Gate maintain a heightened state of vigilance.

Just a short walk beyond the fishing property you'll find the Dauphin Gate, with its manned guardhouse. The gate marks the main entrance by land to the Fortress of Louisbourg.

With each war in Europe, Louisbourg looked uneasily to its neighbours. The British garrison at the Canso fishing base lay a mere 100 km (62 miles) down the coast. Acadia and Newfoundland were both garrisoned by British troops. In wartime, the peaceful New England fishing schooners became armed privateers, scouring the coast for French vessels.

In 1744, the last summer before the siege, sentries at each of the town's gates were especially vigilant. By then, however, the town was in more danger from the spies within the fortress than from those without. Louisbourg was filling up with prisoners taken off New England fishing boats by French privateers. It was the garrison's successful raid on the town of Canso, however, that set in motion the events leading to Louisbourg's capture in 1745.

In the spring of 1744, a fleet of 17 French vessels, carrying just over 300 men, attacked the British colony of Canso. They returned to Louisbourg with over 100 prisoners, including several British officers. These officers witnessed the unrest among the soldiers, shared in the food shortages, and studied the hills that rimmed the town, taking note of the lay of the land. In time, they conveyed their impressions of Louisbourg to Governor William Shirley of Massachusetts, who used the information to plan his attack on the town.

DAUPHIN DEMI-BASTION

To reach the Dauphin Demi-Bastion, pass beyond the guardhouse at the Dauphin Gate, following the wall to a small door. A powder magazine and soldiers' barracks are both located within this stronghold—literally, a fort within a fort. The powder magazine was ingeniously designed, with a vaulted roof to make it bomb-proof. Angled windows ensured that no stray sparks penetrated from the outside.

Up on the wall, the 24-*livres* cannons, arranged in a semi-circle, close off the demi-bastion and protect the harbour. On the landward side, the gun embrasures reveal the long sweep of curtain wall, stretching in a solid line to the King's Bastion. During the first siege, the ground in front of this wall was a deadly no-man's land, swept by crossfire from the Dauphin Demi-Bastion and the King's Bastion beyond.

Both attackers and defenders followed the formal

rules of siege warfare perfected by Sebastien LePrestre de Vauban in the 17th century. A frontal assault was suicidal: the curtain wall was well-protected by steep, earthen outerworks, known as *glacis*. Soldiers who managed to scale these under crossfire from the projecting bastions would still have to cope with the deep ditch and the vertical stone wall. Instead of scaling the walls, besiegers attempted to force a breach at their weakest point, by pounding a hole in the wall with cannon-fire. In Louisbourg, the weakest point was the Dauphin Demi-Bastion. This lowlying bastion was also vulnerable to cannon-fire from the surrounding hills.

The slow, ritual dance of the siege began with Louisbourg's formal refusal to surrender. This was a signal for the New Englanders to begin the long, arduous process of trench-building. Crouching behind a protective barrier of earth, they slowly advanced to within 400 metres (440 yards) of the Dauphin Gate. Three days later, members of the New Hampshire Regiment raised another battery just 230 metres (250 yards) from the gate, roughly where the Desroches House is today. Soon, the earth between these batteries and the Dauphin Demi-Bastion was scorched from the blast of French and New England cannon. Soldiers stationed in the guardhouse just inside the gate desperately piled up rubblestone and earth to reinforce the wall.

As the New Englanders doggedly loaded and reloaded the cannon, they were easy targets for the French soldiers on the wall. By nightfall of the first day, five gunners lay dead. As soon as one gunner fell, another came forward to take his place. Meanwhile, from the far side of the harbour, New England cannon had a clear trajectory to the unprotected walls on the edge of the water. As the days passed, this constant barrage chipped away at the walls of the bastion and the morale of the defenders. Slowly, the Dauphin Gate crumbled under the impact.

In the end, the townspeople were spared the horror of seeing the New Englanders storm the breach in the wall. On the other side of the harbour, a New England battery at Lighthouse Point had overpowered the Island Battery, forcing the French to surrender. The French troops requested and received the honours of war. Shouldering arms, they marched out of the fortress.

POSTERN TUNNEL & QUAY

As you leave the Dauphin Demi-Bastion, you will see a small door in the wall, to your right. This tunnel provided a quick route to the outer defenses. In wartime, soldiers approached the outer works with caution: in the tense summer before the second siege, a militia captain was shot and killed by a nervous soldier on the wall. He had mistaken the officer for an English spy.

Once you have left the Dauphin Demi-Bastion, you have a clear view of the quay to your left. Try to imagine the quay in the summer of 1744, just after the declaration of war in Europe. As usual, Louisbourg Harbour was filled with ships, waiting to load or discharge cargo. Small, three-man fishing shallops delivered boatloads of glistening cod to waiting shoreworkers. Nearby, French square-riggers waited to ship the dried product back to the markets of Europe. Eager merchants inspected the cargoes that had just arrived from France: wool, linen, and damask from French factories, brandy in oak kegs, ceramics, and playing cards.

This year, however, several of the colony's fishing vessels had been converted into armed privateers. These modest ships were critical to the French war effort. A letter of marque from the King gave their captains the authority to seize any vessel belonging to the enemy. With a single penstroke, the French king acquired a

Louisbourg's military installations include the Dauphin Demi-Bastion, the Powder Magazine, and the long curtain wall.

fighting vessel and crew, with no investment on his part.

Most of the privateers attacked unarmed fishing boats, taking a shipload of cod or an assortment of fishing gear. Other prizes were more intriguing. In 1744, François Bauchet de Saint-Martin seized a cargo of coal and 45 Irish girls en route to the American colonies. He could not feed them all, however, and had to let 28 of them go free.

In 1744, Louisbourg also hosted six merchantmen of the *Compagnie des Indes*, en route from India via the Cape of Good Hope. Their captains came to Louisbourg in search of a military escort for the voyage back to France. They were not disappointed. In this last summer before the siege, the frigate *Caribou* and the warship *Ardent* were riding at anchor in the harbour. Altogether, there were about 2600 sailors in the town. They probably spent much of their time in the taverns along the quay, fortifying themselves for the dangerous voyage back to France.

Top right: The harbour in "View from the Clock Tower" by artist Lewis Parker
Bottom: King's storehouse along the quay

LARTIGUE HOUSE & LIME KILN

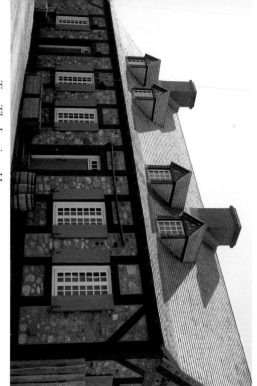

As a seaport, Louisbourg experienced its share of crime. One of the town's most spectacular court cases involved a Basque sailor on one of the fishing vessels. One night in 1740, on the Grand Banks of Newfoundland, a frenzied Bernard Darospide *dit* Detchepart fatally stabbed three of his fellow sailors. Brought to Louisbourg, he was sentenced to be broken on the wheel. To deter others from a similar course, this sentence was to be carried out right on the quay. Following a custom already established in France, authorities would probably have ensured the prisoner was strangled before his limbs were brutally smashed. Although loyal to the letter of the law, Louisbourg authorities had little taste for blood.

This sentence might have been handed down by Joseph Lartigue, *bailli* (town judge) until his death in 1743. His house is the first you encounter after passing through the Dauphin Gate. It is open to the general public as a gift shop operated by the Fortress Louisbourg Association.

*Top: The Lartigue House
Bottom: Sentences handed down by Judge Lartigue varied widely, from mild, public humiliation to capital punishment.*

Lartigue began his career as a simple fishing proprietor, based in Placentia, Newfoundland. His life was a testimony to the opportunities available in Louisbourg. In France, the move from fishing proprietor to merchant to judge was usually achieved over several generations, if at all. Joseph Lartigue achieved it in a single lifetime.

As judge of the *Bailliage* (lower civil and criminal court), Lartigue spent much of his time mediating quarrels between townspeople and settling property disputes. He also tried cases of theft and murder. No one took issue with his lack of legal training. Since his role lay in examining the evidence and questioning the witnesses, the main requirements were literacy and a good understanding of human nature. Any questions of jurisprudence could safely be left to the royal prosecutor.

The *Bailliage* also employed a clerk and a bailiff. Unlike the British colonies to the south, Louisbourg courts had no juries and no defense attorneys. Louis XIV, frustrated with the increasingly high fees charged by French lawyers, had barred lawyers from practicing in the colonies. Instead, witnesses and plaintiffs simply came to Lartigue's house and made a deposition. The presence of Lartigues' twelve children, servants, and washing in the backyard did not detract from Lartigue's dignity. His authority rested in his office, not in the building he occupied.

Once the verdict was handed down, the victim did not linger in jail. Instead, the emphasis was on corporal punishment. Petty theft was usually punishable by whipping or branding on the arm with a "V" for "*Voleur*," or "thief." This brand was useful in identifying repeat offenders.

Lartigue's own sentences were more lenient than those recommended by the royal prosecutor. In one case, the Superior Council (higher court) overturned Lartigue's verdict of whipping, branding and deportation. Instead, the guilty party received a life sentence on the French galleys, all for the theft of a pair of gloves and some money.

Joseph Lartigue spent the last years of his life in this slightly skewed property built just outside the town grid, in the shadow of the fortress wall. One thing marred the peace and prosperity of his final years. The lime kiln situated just behind his house polluted the air with its acrid fumes so that he feared for his health and that of his family. He also worried that a fugitive spark might cause one of his buildings to go up in flames.

The lime kiln was essential to Louisbourg's growth. The limestone was shipped in from quarries in Port Dauphin (Englishtown) and on the Baie des Espagnols (Sydney). Teams of lime-burners tended the huge fires which turned the raw stone into quicklime. Virtually all the town's structures were held together with mortar made from mixing sand and slaked quicklime. Unfortunately, the local limestone contained traces of sandstone, which weakened the mortar. Although builders continually experimented with the formula, masonry structures began to crumble just a few years after their construction.

The lime kiln behind the home of Judge Lartigue was a constant source of frustration.

KING'S BAKERY & FORGES

Courtyard outside the king's bakery

As you leave the Lartigue property, you'll find the king's buildings in the block directly in front of you. The king's buildings—including the artillery storehouse, the King's Bakery and the King's Storehouse farther up the street—were distinguished by their masonry walls and imported slate roofs. Each building was proudly surmounted by the *fleur-de-lis*, symbol of royal presence. Civilian contractors vied for the lucrative contracts.

Some of the buildings suffered from the builders' inexperience with local conditions. For all its status as a royal building, the artillery storehouse was a poorly built structure. The roof leaked, while the floor (built slightly below street level) received the run-off from the ground outside.

A blacksmith's forge was located at one end of the storehouse. The blacksmith was one of Louisbourg's most important artisans. Although all artillery (includ-

ing cannonballs) was imported from France, the blacksmiths were essential to keeping it in good repair. They were equally important in civilian life. The blacksmiths shaped, one by one, the thousands of nails used in the town's construction. Door-hinges, iron hooks and axle-beds all fell into their area of expertise. Today, in the reconstructed forge, visitors can view demonstrations of the blacksmith's craft.

Next to the blacksmith's forge lay the King's Bakery. The baker was also a highly skilled craftsman. Before the invention of baker's yeast in the 19th century, all leavening agents were homemade and highly unstable. Any delay in heating the oven could ruin the bread. As a result, bakers chose their wood carefully, ensuring it caught fire quickly and burned with a steady intensity. Once the embers were swept away, the bread was placed directly on the brick floor of the oven.

The King's Bakery supplied all the bread eaten by the soldiers. Each man received a 6-*livre* loaf that had to

last four days. Unlike the refined white bread eaten by the upper classes, this bread was a hardy mixture of rye and whole wheat flours, milled between two stones. Today, visitors can purchase a small loaf of this soldiers' bread, straight from the ovens.

The bakery staff lived together upstairs, from where they could keep a close eye on the fires. This building also housed the armourer, who repaired the soldiers' muskets and other light arms in his small forge. Extra weapons were stored upstairs. The armoury has not been fully restored and is not open for public viewing.

Top right: Inside the forge
Bottom: Bakers seize a moment of levity in a long, hard day.

DUHAGET & DE LA PÉRELLE HOUSES

Just beside the armoury there is a small gate, which opens onto rue Royale. From here, cross the street to the large, two-storey house to your left. This is the reconstructed house of garrison officer Robert Tarride Duhaget.

Duhaget was a career officer, who typified the slow, sure ascent of a military man in Louisbourg. During the years of peace that followed Louisbourg's founding, young officers did not win promotion through glorious exploits on the battlefield. Instead, they slowly advanced through the ranks by successfully completing a number of administrative duties. During these years, officers spent their time in a routine round of military duties. Some built up a private fortune by investing in the fishery or trade. Duhaget eventually achieved the position of town major, the third highest military rank in Louisbourg after the governor and the *lieutenant de roi*.

When, as a young man, Duhaget built this fine house, he may have been hoping for a large family. However, as there were no children to fill the house, several rooms were rented out as lodging and as government offices. Today, the Duhaget house contains one of several theme lounges on site. The ground floor features an exhibit on Sébastien LePrestre de Vauban and 18th-century methods of siegecraft. The second floor offers a rest area, com-plete with audio-visual presentations and theme-related reading material.

GARDENS: DUHAGET & DE LA PÉRELLE

In any century, it is a struggle to wrest a harvest from the soil of Louisbourg. The growing season is short, its days of sunshine further diminished by the fog that rolls in from the ocean. The thick, sticky clay inhibits drainage.

The back gardens behind the Duhaget and De la Pérelle homes represent the gardens that once graced nearly every home in Louisbourg. In designing the gardens of the reconstruction, park staff turned to a vari-ety of sources. *La nouvelle maison rustique*, published in France in 1755, described the layout of a typical kitchen garden; letters and memoirs of Louisbourg residents re-ferred to the plants grown in the town; and 18th-century cookbooks yielded important information on diet.

Louisbourg's gardens were an important source of fresh food for the townspeople. Cabbage, beans, and carrots added essential nutrients to the inevitable diet of bread and salt fish. Delicate herbs such as parsley and thyme en-hanced a humble bowl of soup. Medicinal plants soothed aching throats and helped staunch a new wound.

These gardens were especially important in years of short-age, when the great warehouses stood empty. Bread was the staple of the French diet in this period. Yet Louisbourg's economy was based on fish, not grain. For basic foodstuffs, Louisbourg looked to the St. Lawrence Valley and cargoes of wheat flour and dried vegetables from France and Acadia.

Trouble arose when French sources failed to provide enough food. In desperation, Louisbourg officials increas-ingly turned to New England, which rarely suffered from crop failure. New England merchants, avid for goods from

Gate leading from the engineer's property affords a fine view of the Duhaget home.

the French sugar islands in the Caribbean, happily supplied the fortress with food. Their ships returned to Boston laden with coffee, sugar, and rum from Louisbourg storehouses.

Unfortunately, this trade fostered an unhealthy dependence on the English. In wartime, the lack of New England food supplies seriously weakened the fortress. Long before the outbreak of war, Louisbourg administrators looked for ways to increase the colony's self-sufficiency. Enterprising colonists were encouraged to carve out meadows along the banks of the Mira River. Their hay would serve as fodder for Ile Royale cattle.

Unfortunately, the output of the Mira farms remained small. Louisbourg's settlers were fishermen and artisans, not stock handlers. In desperation, the administrators tried to induce Acadian farmers to settle in Ile Royale. All along the Bay of Fundy, Acadians were raising cattle on salt marsh hay. Their barns were filled to bursting with grain. Yet few Acadians wished to trade their rich lands for the rocky soil of Ile Royale.

The shortage of food was one reason for the attack on Canso in 1744. A year earlier, Louisbourg officials had purchased emergency rations from the British at Canso. The declaration of war in 1744 removed that option. Now, New England privateers cruising stealthily off the coast kept even the French supply ships from reaching Louisbourg. The governor felt that the town's only hope lay in retaking Acadia. The first step was to remove the garrison at Canso.

Some of the prisoners taken at Canso were housed in Major de la Pérelle's warehouse. Like his neighbour Du-haget, de la Pérelle had served as town major. In addition, his role as English interpreter to the Governor provided him with a welcome supplement to his military income.

De la Pérelle does not seem to have spent the summer of 1744 in his home, but lived in a rented house elsewhere in town. Perhaps he did not want to share the property with prisoners of war. Today, the De la Pérelle house has an exhibit about the Sisters of the Congregation of Notre Dame who operated a school for girls in Louisbourg.

Top: De la Pérelle house
Bottom: Small gardens such as these greatly enhanced the citizens' chances of survival.

ENGINEER'S RESIDENCE

The large masonry house across the street from the De la Pérelle home belonged to Étienne Verrier, *ingénieur du roi*. Unlike many of his fellow officers, Étienne Verrier was not a member of the nobility. His father and great-uncle were both sculptors in Aix-en-Provence, France. Although Verrier had inherited their artistic talent, he was not encouraged to follow in their footsteps. In the 18th century, successful artisans positioned their sons to enter the professional class or the merchant class. Young Étienne joined the highly trained, professional corps of military engineers.

Étienne Verrier was 41 years old when he arrived in Louisbourg. A year later, in 1724, he was promoted to the post of *ingénieur du roi*. Verrier designed the Dauphin Demi-Bastion, the Island Battery and the Royal Battery. He also designed most of the public buildings in the town, including the hospital, the government storehouse, the bakery, and the main gates.

Verrier spared no expense in constructing his own official residence; his superiors grumbled about a mere engineer having such a stately home. (As with most of his projects, Verrier had underestimated the amount of official funds necessary for construction.) Verrier's wife had come out briefly in 1732, but returned to France after only three years. For most of his stay, Verrier lived here with just his son—also an engineer—and a few servants. Verrier's son, known as the Chevalier Verrier, had inherited the artistic talents of his father and grandfather. He produced one of the best-known contemporary drawings of the town.

Top: Servant in the engineer's kitchen
Bottom: The large home of military engineer Étienne Verrier stood as a physical reminder of his status.

ENGINEER'S RESIDENCE

Top: *Engineer Verrier ponders the strength of Louisbourg's fortifications.*
Middle: *Chairs pushed against the wall in a summer arrangement.*
Bottom: *In its small way, the engineer's garden imitates the formality of Versailles.*

The engineer's residence was a centre of activity in Louisbourg. A constant stream of contractors, military officers and administrators visited Verrier's office at the rear of the house. As one of the highest-ranking officials, it is likely that Verrier also did his share of official entertaining. Card parties, banquets, and musical evenings helped alleviate the isolation of life in a military outpost.

Outside, the carefully-groomed garden paths were perfect for promenades. Gardening was a passion of the age, and most well-educated people claimed some knowledge of the art. The plants were, for the most part, the hardiest of vegetables. Yet Verrier's guests would have found much to admire in the skillful blend of colours and the placement of fragrant herbs so near the path. Like most French gardens of the period, this one owed its inspiration to the formal gardens of the palaces and *chateaux* of France, where beds were laid out with mathematical precision.

This same precision was applied to the layout of the town itself. Throughout North America, military engineers were designing straight thoroughfares and dividing towns into blocks. Likewise, in 1717, Louisbourg's royal engineers zealously reorganized all town properties along a grid system. Few people were permitted to destroy the perfect symmetry of these lines. If existing homes lay across grid lines, their owners were encouraged to tear them down.

Slowly, the sprawling fishing village within Louisbourg's walls became a tidy, compact town. Townspeople discovered that many aspects of their daily lives were now in the hands of the professionals. A professional surveyor measured all boundary lines. A host of ordinances dictated that property owners develop empty lots, pen their animals in back yards, and clear the ice away from their homes. This was a long way from the easy freedom of the early years.

For his part, Verrier had the satisfaction of seeing a modern town spring up before his eyes. He also lived to see much of his work destroyed in the siege of 1745. Our last glimpse of Verrier is in a council of war, persuading the French commanders not to blow up the Royal Battery, one of his own designs. This was a mistake. Shortly after, the English captured the Battery and turned its guns on the town.

Top: Rodrigue warehouse
Bottom: Michel Rodrigue's commercial success resulted in this imposing home.

The warehouse located just across the street from the Verrier property belonged to the Rodrigue family. They lived in the large house on the corner of rue Toulouse and rue Royale. Michel Rodrigue had arrived in Louisbourg as a child of seven, part of the original group of Placentia settlers.

Shipping was in his blood. His father had been born in Portugal, the maritime nation that produced some of the greatest pilots in the world. After emigrating to North America, the elder Rodrigue became ship's pilot in Port Royal. In Placentia, he acquired a fleet of fishing vessels.

Young Michel began his career as a pilot at his father's side. In 1732, at the age of 25, he was given his own command, sailing the family brigantine, *La Revanche*. He travelled to Quebec and as far as the French colonies of the Caribbean. (Louisbourg's cod kept well in the tropical climate of Martinique and St. Domingue, and was a staple of the plantation diet. Even today, salt fish plays an important role in Caribbean cooking.)

On the return voyage north, the ships' holds were loaded with coffee, sugar, and rum. These goods were

warehoused in Louisbourg for shipment to France or Quebec. This intercolonial trade did not interfere with the French trade. In fact, French sea captains preferred to leave goods destined for Quebec in Louisbourg, rather than make the lengthy trip up the St. Lawrence. The Rodrigue ships were a familiar sight on the great river, bringing French fashions, wine, and other goods to the people of Quebec. On the return voyage, they shipped Canadian flour and dried peas to the colonists of Ile Royale. Many of these foodstuffs were stored in Rodrigue's warehouse, located adjacent to his house.

By the age of 30, Michel Rodrigue was one of Louisbourg's most successful businessmen. Married and the father of a growing family, he left the active sailing to his two brothers, Pierre and Antoine. The large house on rue Royale became the command centre of a thriving family firm, with Michel Rodrigue at its head.

Luckily, the firm's profits were safely invested in France. When Louisbourg fell for the first time, the family simply moved its base of operations to La Rochelle on the west coast of France. Michel's two brothers returned to Louisbourg after the war. It was common practice for French trading houses to send an agent to Louisbourg to oversee the sale of goods shipped from Europe. Pierre and Antoine Rodrigue represented their brother's interests. Antoine also captained the fine ships outfitted by Michel's firm in France. These were chartered to local officials in Louisbourg.

Before long, Michel Rodrigue's shipping empire extended to French colonies throughout the world. By 1764, his fortune allowed him to purchase the office of Treasurer in La Rochelle's Bureau of Finance, with its attendant noble status. Michel Rodrigue had finally won the greatest prize of all. The man who had begun his career piloting the small coastal vessels of Ile Royale ended his life as a member of the French nobility.

Top: Rodrigue outbuildings
Bottom: Ground herbs offered zest to a limited diet.

DE GANNES HOUSE

The small house at the top of the hill, to your right, is the reconstructed house of Michel de Gannes de Falaise, Captain in the *Compagnies franches de la Marine*. Michel de Gannes was born in Port Royal, where his father was an officer in the garrison. The de Gannes family originated in the French province of Poitou and its ancestry reached back to the 14th century. On his mother's side, Michel was descended from the same le Neuf family which produced a governor of Acadia.

Michel de Gannes was 20 years old when he arrived in Louisbourg in 1722. Ties of kinship and marriage already united him to Louisbourg's close-knit elite, most of whom were also born in North America. As members of the elite, Louisbourg's officers were expected to live in a manner consistent with their high status. Yet, in spite of their noble birth, few officers possessed inherited wealth and their small military salaries did not cover their expenses, which included fine clothing, a house in town, and frequent appearances at the gaming tables.

In Louisbourg, however, a shrewd and ambitious man did not remain poor for long. Construction and trade were booming, and few officers could resist the chance to participate. De Gannes himself derived a small income from property rentals. The wealthy Rodrigue family leased de Gannes' substantial house in Block 17. By the 1740s, he and Antoine Rodrigue were co-owners of a schooner, the *Salamandre*.

By our standards, Michel de Gannes' house does not look like the home of a prosperous military officer. In contrast, his Rodrigue property is a far more imposing residence. De Gannes' choice of the humbler home suggests a certain prudence in the management of his financial affairs. Historians have also speculated that de Gannes' snugly built, wooden home was probably far warmer than the

*Top: De Gannes house
Bottom: Lace-making firmly entrenched Madame de Gannes' status as a military wife.*

spacious, stone houses of his neighbours.

This small house sheltered de Gannes, his wife, Elisabeth de Catalogne, and seven children. In obedience to a court order, de Gannes was also supporting another child, conceived when he was a young, unmarried lieutenant.

Each room in the house probably served a variety of purposes. Louisbourg residents would have accepted without question the presence of a bed in the parlour, or salon. By 18th-century standards, the heavy curtains assured an acceptable degree of privacy for the bed's occupants. Even when the parents retired for the night, other family members might use the room for letter writing, study, or entertaining.

The children's sleeping arrangements were far more casual. Trundle beds, designed to slide under a larger bed, conserved space during the day. Small corners were boarded in to serve as sleeping alcoves. Older children probably slept in the attic, sharing the space with winter food supplies.

In most homes, family life centred on the kitchen, with its warm fire. Wooden walkers kept toddlers away from the flames. These walkers were similar to those we use today, with the exception that the wheels limited the child's movement to one direction only.

As a high-ranking military wife, Madame de Gannes probably left many of the household tasks to servants. Lace-making, entertaining, and instructing her daughters were considered more appropriate activities for a lady.

In the end, war destroyed de Gannes' efforts to build a secure future in Ile Royale. After the siege of 1745, the family was sent to France, with the rest of the town's occupants. When they returned in 1749, de Gannes was promoted to town major, the third highest military rank after the governor and king's lieutenant. Michel de Gannes did not live to see Louisbourg's final fall. He died in 1752, at the age of 50, and was interred beneath the chapel floor.

Top: Servant in the de Gannes kitchen
Middle: A walker kept toddlers from straying too close to the fire.
Bottom: The marital bed held pride of place in the de Gannes home.

ICE HOUSE & GUARDHOUSE

The cone-shaped building just behind de Gannes' house was the ice house. Winter ice, cut from the ponds and hauled to the town in sledges, was set inside the structure's deep pit and carefully packed in straw. The pointed roof had no flat surfaces to hold the sun's heat, while the north-facing door was opened only before dawn or after sunset. The *fleur-de-lis* at the top meant that the ice house was a king's building. The luxury of iced drinks was available only to those who enjoyed the governor's hospitality or his patronage.

From the ice house, retrace your steps to the walkway located in front of the De Gannes house. The guardhouse lies beyond the walkway, just inside the wall. The soldiers mustered for roll call and the changing of the guard in the Place d'Armes, located directly in front of the guardhouse.

The townspeople of Louisbourg went to bed at night knowing they were protected. The guard-houses at the gates of the town set firm barriers be-tween them and the wilderness that lay just beyond the town and its harbour. The tramp of the night watch and the sound of morning drumbeats were comforting reminders of a military presence.

This guardhouse is one of five that were located within the town. The others were at the Dauphin Gate, the Queen's Gate, the Maurepas Gate, and the Pièce de la Grave. The Island and Royal batter-ies each had their own guard as well.

Each 24-hour guard detail was divided into three shifts. Every soldier spent a total of eight hours on sentry duty, usually served in two-hour blocks of time. The remaining two eight-hour shifts were spent sleeping and on call, performing odd jobs for the officers.

Top: The ice house sheltered straw-wrapped blocks of winter ice.
Bottom: A soldier whiles away long hours of sentry duty.

The guard also comprised the town's police force. At night, patrols of soldiers thrust their lamps into dark corners and peered into back yards. Too often, they encountered one of their own comrades in the act of performing a crime. As a port town with a large migrant population, Louisbourg attracted its share of idlers and adventurers. Yet, of all the people who landed on Louisbourg's shores, the soldiers themselves were among the most desperate. Socially, their status was well below that of the artisan. Even the servants looked down on them. The soldiers were probably feared and perhaps even despised by most of the women of the town. With little hope of marrying and raising a family, the soldiers spent their free time in the taverns along the quay.

Fights and break-ins often followed a night of drinking on the town. When this happened, civilians found themselves in the *Bailliage*, soldiers in a military court. Drunken or insubordinate soldiers were sometimes sentenced to sit astride two narrow boards, cut to resemble a horse. Passers-by jeered as the offender sat there for several painful hours, his legs weighted and his hands bound.

Aside from these fairly minor offenses, life in Louisbourg progressed quite peaceably. In such a small community, the fear of ostracism was a powerful force in curbing anti-social behaviour. The church also exerted a beneficial influence on the conduct of the townspeople, who were for the most part Roman Catholic.

Right: Drummer with the Compagnies franches de la Marine
Bottom: Inside the guardhouse at the Dauphin Gate

CHAPEL

Louisbourg's small chapel is located to your left in the huge barracks building just beyond the drawbridge. The relationship between the Church and State is best expressed by historian Guy Frégault, who claimed, "The men of the State were Catholics; the men of the Church served the State." Louisbourg's governor occupied a place of honour to the right of the altar. In the reconstructed chapel, a picture of St. Louis (King of France in the 13th century) hangs over the altar. The symbolism would not have been lost on the townspeople. French society was based on two fixed realities: God in His Heaven and the king on his throne.

Still, in Louisbourg, the church did not wield the power it exerted elsewhere. Ile Royale was just one of many missions in the vast Diocese of Quebec. In Quebec, the bishop was a member of the *Conseil Supérieur* and therefore had a voice in shaping government policy. In contrast, no bishop sat on Louisbourg's *Conseil Supérieur*. Louisbourg's clergy owned no vast lands or impressive buildings. When town administrators suggested imposing a tithe on the cod fishery for the establishment of a

Catholicism held out promises of protection and structure in an uncertain world.

Top: Confessional
Bottom: Details from the chapel interior

parish church, the townspeople vigorously resisted. They continued to worship in the small military chapel.

The Louisbourg parish was known as Our Lady of Angels. As a mission, it fell under the care of the Recollets, a branch of the Franciscan order, whose priests came from Brittany. There were usually four Recollet priests serving in Louisbourg. One lived in the small room just behind the chapel, while the others lived in the Recollet convent in town. The fathers' lack of learning exasperated the Bishops of Quebec; the townspeople, however, appreciated their simple faith. They also respected the Recollets' willingness to share the hardships and joys of their parishioners. The Recollet fathers presided at baptisms, weddings, and funerals. They frequently mediated in family or community disputes. When Marie-Anne Carrerot found herself pregnant by Michel de Gannes, she asked the parish priest to persuade the reluctant officer to marry her. Although de Gannes married another, he agreed to support the child.

For the people of Louisbourg, Sunday mass was a social, as well as a spiritual, event. The 37 holy days of obligation provided further opportunity for services, promenades, and feasting. On state holidays and after military victories, the Recollet fathers organized processions through the streets of the town.

In contrast, the few resident Protestants were excluded from full participation in the life of the town. Official intolerance was common in most 18th-century communities, Catholic and Protestant alike. In Louisbourg, for example, Protestants were barred from holding public posts. Their isolation was doubtless compounded by the absence of Protestant women of marriageable age. Even the town's cemeteries were closed to them.

The most prestigious burial ground in the city was just beneath the chapel floor. Governor de Forant was buried there in 1740, followed four years later by Governor du Quesnel. Beside them lies the Duc d'Enville, leader of the ill-fated expedition to reclaim Louisbourg in 1746. Captain de Gannes also received the honour of burial beneath the chapel. During the reconstruction in the 1960s, their skeletons were excavated, then carefully covered up again.

GOVERNOR'S WING

Once inside the gate, after leaving the chapel, turn left and enter the first door you encounter. These are the living quarters for the governor and some of his officers. Between 1713 and 1759, Louisbourg knew five governors. All were members of the French military aristocracy. Only one commander of Ile Royale, Louis du Chambon, was promoted from within the local officer corps. When Governor du Quesnel died late in 1744, du Chambon assumed command until a new governor could be sent out from France; before that happened, however, the British came.

Although the governor represented the King of France, he did not reign supreme in Ile Royale. His authority was tempered by the chief financial administrator, known as the *commissaire-ordonnateur*. Each official had his own sphere of influence. The governor

Top: Detail of faïence basin
Below: Conseil Supérieur, Louisbourg's seat of government

oversaw the management of the garrison and the state of the fortifications. He also presided over diplomatic relations with New England and relations with France's native allies, the Mi'kmaq. The *commissaire-ordonnateur* controlled the treasury and regulated all matters of trade and finance. As head of provisioning, he encouraged the local production of foodstuffs and the development of coal-mining in the area.

Both the governor and the *commissaire-ordonnateur* were responsible to the French *Ministère de la Marine*, and the two officials shared many duties. Both served on the *Conseil Supérieur*. Until the establishment of the *Bailliage* in 1734, the *Conseil Supérieur* had been the sole civil and criminal court. Afterwards, it functioned as the court of appeal. The *commissaire-ordonnateur* presided over its Saturday morning meetings, held in the ornate room beneath the governor's apartments. The two officials also served on the *conseil de guerre*, a court martial convened only in the event of a serious military

Right: Governor's bed
Below: The Governor's writing desk reflects the French passion for objets d'art.

As the King's representative, the Governor dressed in a manner befitting his status.

crime. Obviously, this shared authority worked best when the two senior officials put aside professional jealousies and focused on developing the colony. By 1740, the two offices were working as a team. When Governor du Quesnel arrived in that year to take office, the colony's future seemed assured.

Jean-Baptiste Louis LePrévost du Quesnel was an old war horse whose devotion to France had cost him a leg. Du Quesnel conceived and directed the only two attacks ever launched from Louisbourg: the capture of Canso in 1744 and the aborted attack on Annapolis Royal later that summer. At his death, the fortress fell under the command of du Chambon, an Ile Royale veteran whose abilities had never been tried in battle.

In furnishing Governor du Quesnel's apartments, historians relied on an inventory of his possessions, made at

the time of his death in 1744. As the representatives of the King of France, Louisbourg's governors were expected to make an impressive show. France, after all, was not simply a military power; it was the centre of culture, art, fashion and cuisine. At a time when France and England were locked in a struggle to control North America, France marshalled all its forces to the cause. Not least among these was a firm belief in its ability to civilize a raw land. Accordingly, the governor's apartments were decorated with fine objects accumulated over a long career. Guests were treated to subtle French wines and delicate savouries, served on crisp linen. The conversation was at once polished and spiced. In the end, however, it was force that decided the fate of North America. In 1758, British artillery shells crashed into the King's Bastion, destroying the chapel, the barracks, and France's hopes of controlling the east coast.

The small enclosure outside this wing sheltered the animals that belonged to the governor's household. The two-storey grey building is a dovecote. From here, follow the pathway that leads up to the ramparts. (In the interests of safety, visitors are forbidden to stand on the grassy tops of the ramparts. Please be especially cautious with children.)

RAMPARTS

Opposite the *Conseil Supérieur* and the governor's apartments are the ramparts. In both sieges, the attacking forces set up gun batteries on the low hills just beyond the ramparts. Even in the early years, Louisbourg's designers were uncomfortably aware of the fortress' vulnerability to an attack from this direction. Yet beyond lowering the hills, or extending the fortifications out to cover the entire peninsula, there was little they could do. They felt, in any case, that several kilometres of swamp and brush would deter any attempts to mount a land attack. They were wrong.

From the top of the ramparts, you can look out beyond the boggy, wooded hills to the waters of Gabarus Bay. The attackers landed their ships in one of its small coves, just down the coast. For several days, they hauled their cannons through the viscous mud of early spring to a campsite situated on the banks of a small brook.

In the first siege in 1745, most of the fighting force came from Massachusetts, which supplied seven of the nine infantry regiments. Connecticut and New Hampshire each supplied one regiment. New York supplied some artillery, while Rhode Island's contribution came in the form of a small colonial warship. The colonial soldiers, largely militia, had never seen a proper Vauban fortress armed by regular soldiers. Louisbourg's walls, looming solid and grey before them, might have seemed impenetrable. The French, on the other hand, were only too aware of the stone's vulnerability. The mighty walls, just recently completed, were already crumbling from the freeze-thaw cycles and the eroding effects of salt air on mortar. Soon, they would succumb to the shattering blows of New England cannons.

According to Vauban's theory, the defender's strategy was to keep the attackers at bay until help arrived in the form of warships from France. Unfortunately, the anticipated help never came. The two ships sent to protect Louisbourg during the first siege never made it through the blockade. In the second siege in 1758, the five French warships stationed in Louisbourg were trapped in the harbour, where they mounted a listless defense against the gun batteries mounted by British general James Wolfe. Without adequate naval support, the soldiers on the walls were fighting a losing battle. France's inability to provide a strong naval presence in Louisbourg has been cited as an important reason for the fortress' fall.

From the ramparts, descend to the courtyard. The large rooms in the wall to your left are known as casemates.

The soldiers' efforts could not compensate for the structural deficiencies in Louisbourg's design.

39

Raising domestic animals provided the citizens with some relief from a steady diet of cod.

Although generally used for storage, they sheltered the townspeople from artillery fire during the sieges.

From here, proceed to the soldiers' barrack rooms, located directly in front of you. The lower floor of this wing houses an exhibit on the reconstruction process and archaeology. Visitors' washrooms are also located on the lower floor, to your extreme left. Part of the upper floor is furnished as soldiers' barracks.

SOLDIERS' BARRACKS

For many soldiers, defending the fortress was the final act in a short and desolate life. How did they come to this end? For hundreds of poor young men in France, the simple promise of another meal was enough to lure them across the ocean. Others were enticed with alcohol, the victims of unscrupulous recruiters. Most had agreed to an "*engagement perpetuel,*" which meant they entertained little hope of seeing France for quite some time.

Most of Louisbourg's soldiers wore the blue uniform and grey-white coat of the *Compagnies franches de la Marine*. They were small: to fill the ranks, colonial recruiters often had to overlook the five foot, four inch, minimum height requirement. Some were as young as 16 years of age, while others were sickly or malnourished. Less than half could sign their names. It was not an elite unit!

The recruits assigned to Louisbourg did not fare badly. They were not exposed to the tropical fevers that killed so

many French soldiers in the Caribbean. Unlike the small British garrison in Nova Scotia, the Louisbourg soldiers did not fear the possibility of an attack by native people: the local Mi'kmaq were firm allies of the French. For the first 31 years of its existence, Louisbourg was a peaceful, prosperous trading town.

The most daunting task which faced the recruits was building the fortifications. Even this provided the diversion of challenging work and the opportunity to earn extra money. In fact, any soldier who preferred stone-masonry to guard duty could pay another to take his place in the sentry box.

In Louisbourg, the soldiers lived in the King's Bastion Barracks, one of the first barracks to be built in North America. When not on guard duty, they slept 15–20 to a room, two to a bed. It was a life lived in the constant company of over 600 other men. Some soldiers seized a few moments of solitude by escaping to the woods with musket and dogs. There, they hunted small game to sell, or to round out official rations. In addition to the bread ration, the soldiers received four ounces of salt meat per day, with four ounces of dried peas and beans. Back in the barracks, seven or eight men pooled these rations into a single, thick stew.

In addition to hunting, the soldiers foraged for berries, shellfish, and the eggs of sea birds. Spruce beer could be had for free by boiling together the tender tips of spruce boughs with the monthly ration of molasses. The natives had taught the first settlers how to make this brew. Today we know that its high content of ascorbic acid prevented the dreaded disease known as scurvy (*scorbut*).

In the early years, the soldiers earned enough to buy an occasional meal and a bottle of rum in one of the taverns. Inevitably, however, the acquisitive eyes of the officers fell upon these earnings. By the 1730s, the men's wages were being paid directly to the officers. With no cash in their pocket, the soldiers were forced to buy on credit in the military canteens, at usurious rates. They received the balance of their wages at the end of the year. Too often, there was nothing left.

As conditions continued to deteriorate, the men grew more restless. The mutiny of 1744 began with the soldiers in the Swiss Karrer Regiment. It was fatally easy to organize: under the new barracks system, all the men were under one roof.

The Karrer Regiment held a somewhat privileged position within the Louisbourg soldier. By 1744, the Louisbourg contingent was comprised of about 150 soldiers, all from small Swiss and German states. Unlike the grey-coated soldiers of the *Compagnies franches de la Marine*, the soldiers of the Karrer regiment wore striking red coats with royal blue cuffs, and blue vests with white stripes. These soldiers had the option of leaving the services after six years. Their professional pride rebelled against the treatment they were forced to endure in Louisbourg.

The mutiny began quietly. Two days after Christmas, at 6:00 a.m., most of the garrison assembled in the parade ground. Only the elite unit of *Canonier bombardiers* (cannoneers) remained aloof.

As the soldiers stood quietly in the parade ground, their leaders presented their list of grievances. In that year of food shortages, the officers had sold their vegetable rations to the townspeople, while distributing the rotten remains to the barracks. That summer, Governor du Quesnel had promised a share of the booty to all soldiers who participated in the attack on Canso. By October, du Quesnel was

dead and the booty, largely salted cod, had disappeared.

Although the mutiny began peacefully enough, it ended with ugly threats and brandishing of arms. The uneasy relations between the officers and their men continued until the siege of 1745. The men fought bravely, confident in the governor's assurance of a full pardon. The pardon was later revoked by the *Ministère de la Marine*, who blamed the soldiers for Louisbourg's fate. He claimed that word of their unrest (conveyed by English prisoners) had inspired Governor Shirley to risk an attack. Eventually, eight men were executed for their part in the mutiny: three from the Karrer Regiment and five from the *Compagnies franches de la Marine*.

As you leave the King's Bastion and look away from the drawbridge to the ocean beyond, you will notice a building of grey stone, constructed differently from the others. This is the first museum, built on the site in 1936. Its history and a brief introduction to its exhibits are provided in the section of this book entitled "Reconstruction." The walled square marks the site of the king's garden, once thick with root vegetables and herbs.

Far from home and spurned by townspeople, the soldier endured a hard life.

Top: De la Plagne house
Below: Delicate iron tracery shows the French love of detail.

From the king's garden, proceed across the parade ground (known as the Place Royale) to the large, yellow De la Plagne house on the corner of rue Royale. This spacious house contains an exhibit on the history and culture of the Mi'kmaq. The exhibit also has seating for visitors.

This house was only five years old in 1744. It was built by Company Captain Pierre-Paul d'Espiet de la Plagne, who inherited the land from an uncle. De la Plagne's own impeccable status notwithstanding, the property itself has a somewhat lurid history. In 1725, a soldier working in the garden fell into a well and drowned. In 1740, a former soldier named La Fleur, who had once been employed in the house, returned to steal some silver coins. The *Conseil Supérieur* sentenced him to a lifetime on the French galleys.

Along the street from the De la Plagne house lies the property of Louis le Neuf de la Vallière. Many of the houses in this prestigious part of town belonged to high-ranking military officers. Louis le Neuf de la Vallière was a cousin of Michel de Gannes. He had been born in

Placentia and was brought to Louisbourg as a small child. He was one of the few people of French descent who could speak Mi'kmaq, the language of France's native allies.

De la Vallière acquitted himself well in the attack on Canso in 1744, and in the summer before the siege, he was sent to France to report the victory. His pregnant wife remained at home with their small daughter and several of Louis' siblings.

During the siege, de la Vallière commanded a company posted to the Maurepas Bastion. After the war, he was one of the Louisbourg residents who refused to relinquish the only home he had ever known. He returned to the town in 1749 and remained there until its fall in 1758. Later, he commanded a garrison in French Guyana. De la Vallière's spacious warehouses are located just behind his house. The stone *pavé* floors date back to the original 18th-century structures.

Right: Goods in the De la Vallière warehouse
Below: Louis le Neuf de la Vallière built himself a fine private home.

Brought to Canada by the French, invasive Angelica plants encroach upon the Loppinot ruins.

LOPPINOT/FIZEL RUINS & DUGAS/DE LA TOUR HOUSE

Just behind the second De la Vallière storehouse lie the excavated ruins of the Loppinot property. Jean Chrysostome Loppinot was one of Louis le Neuf de la Vallière's fellow officers. This was another crowded family home, housing Loppinot and his wife, their eight children, and a servant. There, too, lived Loppinot's slave, Marie Marguerite Rose, and her son, Jean François.

It was a time when few people reflected on the morality of slave-holding. Unlike the Caribbean islands, with their large sugar and coffee plantations, Louisbourg did not have a slave economy. Still, slaves were looked upon as a commodity and traded in Louisbourg. Schooners sailing to the Antilles often brought back slaves for the homeowners of Louisbourg.

The number of slaves in a household enhanced the status of the owner. Most of Louisbourg's governors and *commissaires-ordonnateur* were slave owners. In all, there were at least 363 slaves on Ile Royale, with the great majority working in Louisbourg as domestics. The Lartigue, Benoist, Grandchamp, and Dugas families, among others, all owned slaves. The Brothers of Charity, the order

that ran the hospital, returned to Ile Royale in 1749 with four slaves. The Rodrigue household on rue Toulouse also housed a Native slave, Marguerite. In New France, all Native slaves were known as *Panis* (Pawnee), although not all Native slaves were members of that tribe. There were 18 *Panis* slaves in Louisbourg's history. Loppinot's slave, Marie Marguerite Rose, obtained her freedom in 1755, just before marrying. Until her death in 1757, she and her husband operated a tavern just up the street. Her son, Jean François, died in 1751, at the age of 13.

Loppinot's neighbour, Julien Fizel, ran an inn. Fizel was busily engaged in most of the lucrative activities in Louisbourg. He owned a fishing property in the Faux-bourg and land for pasturing livestock. He also bought and sold ships. A militia captain, Fizel died when he was accidentally shot by a nervous French soldier who mistook him for an English spy.

After Louisbourg fell to the English in 1758, the fortifications were blown up. However, many of the houses were left standing and were subsequently occupied by British members of the garrison. This was the fate of the Fizel house until it was destroyed in a fire in 1762. For archaeologists, a house that is destroyed by fire represents a sort of time capsule. Features such as walls, chimneys, and drains remain as they were at the moment of destruction, unspoiled by the addition of later structures. Objects that could not be salvaged from the fire are simply left in the ruins. The blackened stone is not carted away for construction, but remains on the site. In destroying the Fizel house, the fire preserved the evidence of it forever.

DUGAS/DE LA TOUR HOUSE

The twin-gabled duplex located across the street from the Loppinot/Fizel and Loppinot properties is known as the "Dugas/ De la Tour House." Today, it serves as office space for park staff and is closed to the public. In the 18th century, however, the property belonged to Marguerite Richard and Charles Saint-Etienne de la Tour. De la Tour was an officer in the garrison and the grandson of Charles de la Tour, one of the most famous figures in Acadia's history. It was a proud name and a proud heritage.

De la Tour was Marguerite Richard's second husband. Their marriage was a good example of the upward mobility available to women in Louisbourg. With men outnumbering women by as much as eight to one in the early years, an unattached woman could often marry above her class. Marguerite Richard's first husband, Joseph Dugas, had been a carpenter. Although not in the same league as de la Tour, Dugas was a highly respected artisan. In fact, his skill brought him a fine, duplex house in this good section of town. He had originally been contracted to build the house for Dominique Detcheverry, a Basque

blacksmith. In return, Detcheverry gave him half the house as payment.

These two men, Dugas and Detcheverry, were sturdy representatives of the working class that had converted Louisbourg from a mere fishing station into a real town. Carpenters and blacksmiths were among the first wave of artisans to settle in a new area, along with coopers, bricklayers and wheelwrights. They established the small shops, filled with helpers and apprentices, that formed the basis of production in the 18th century.

As their children grew, they were brought into the business. Very small children were given the simplest tasks to perform. A young Dugas might have begun by sweeping up wood shavings in the shop. Artisans also sent their children out to apprentice in other, related businesses. A carpenter's son who served a seven-year apprenticeship with a blacksmith brought skills to the family business so that the father no longer needed to contract out for iron fittings such as hinges and doorlocks.

Dugas/De la Tour house

45

CARREROT & BENOIST HOUSES

As the keeper of the King's Warehouse, or chief clerk, André Carrerot was a high-ranking member of Louisbourg's civil bureaucracy. The Carrerots' fine house on the corner of rue Royale and rue Toulouse sheltered André, his wife Marguerite-Thérèse, and their 10 children. Their home was typical of well-to-do residents in Louisbourg. Once Louisbourg was declared the capital of Ile Royale in 1720, families began to plan for the future. Newly prosperous settlers abandoned the single-storey, pole-and-mortar type of construction known as *piquet* in favour of more substantial homes.

Today, the Carrerot home houses an exhibition on 18th-century building techniques. The structure was built in the style known as *charpente* (half-timber). It began with a frame built entirely of thick, squared timbers. These were fitted together using mortise and tenon joints, carefully cut into each end of the wood. Hand-crafted wooden pins held the joint in place. In the early years, the local builders fashioned both timber and pins. As trade with New England stepped up, however, contractors began purchasing Boston board. Some even imported pre-fabricated frames, their joints marked for quick assembly.

The fill depended on the financial status of the homeowner. *Piquet* fill was the most economical choice, since the builder simply placed the wooden poles within the timber frame and then filled in the spaces with mortar. Alternatively, logs could be placed horizontally one on top of the other, in a style known as *pièce sur pièce*. Masonry fill was more expensive. When New England brick became available, the spaces between the timbers displayed intricately-laid patterns. As you walk along the far end of the quay, explore the various examples of brick fill in some of the reconstructed buildings.

Top: Carrerot house
Left: Piquet construction offered a snug, warm shelter from the elements.

For extra warmth, some houses were covered in boards, inside and out. The exterior wooden covering also protected the mortar from the corrosive effects of the fog and salt air. Every family had to decide for itself how far it was willing to compromise warmth for fashion. Captain de Gannes had opted for a small, *piquet* house, sheathed tightly in boards. The engineer Verrier, on the other hand, chose high ceilings and elegant (if cold) stone. As the colony became more prosperous, the townspeople began importing window glass, which was then cut into a number of tiny panes and fit into a latticed wooden frame, using glued paper. Outside, wooden shutters were effective barriers against the night and the blowing snow.

Louisbourg builders were aware of the fine, blowing snow known as *poudrerie* (powder) that insinuated itself into tiny cracks and crevices. Hand-shaped shingles were firmly nailed onto closely bevelled roofboards. Steeply pitched roofs kept the snow from settling, while flaring eaves swept it back into the street.

Even the best-made roofs, however, were not resistant to cannon balls. The Carrerot house was hit twice during the first siege. Lieutenant Pierre Benoist's small house next door was destroyed. The shots were lobbed from the New England batteries located just outside the Dauphin Demi-Bastion.

The Benoist House is not open to the public, but serves

as an administrative building. In 1745, the property was owned by Pierre Benoist, commander of the French fortifications at Port Toulouse (St. Peter's, Nova Scotia). A widower, Benoist had lost his wife and young daughter to the smallpox epidemic of 1732-1733.

(A washroom located across the street from the Benoist House can be reached through the small door in the stone wall.)

Top: Louisbourg houses reflect the Norman heritage of their builders.

Bottom: Even in this most remote corner of France, artisans took pride in their work.

À L'ÉPÉE ROYALE, HÔTEL DE LA MARINE & GRANDCHAMPS INN

Top: À l'Épée Royale offers travelers the choice of fine dining.
Above: A friendly game at Grandchamps Inn

Adjacent to the Benoist House, a sign marks the location of the inn known as À l'Épée Royale. Jean Seigneur, a widower, ran the original inn with the help of his daughter, Françoise. Guests slept in the half storey upstairs. Next door on the quay, the Hôtel de la Marine and its neighbour, the Grandchamps Inn, also welcomed paying guests. Today the Fortress Louisbourg Association operates all three properties as period restaurants, providing the same food and drink that were available long ago. A non-profit society, the Fortress Louisbourg Association uses the proceeds to fund interpretive and educational projects.

À l'Épée Royale is a modest building compared with its fine masonry neighbour, the Hôtel de la Marine, yet the Hôtel de la Marine was the humbler of the two. In contrast, À l'Épée Royale served a more exacting clientele. In its dining room, prosperous merchants and visiting sea captains sampled imported wines and dishes prepared to their discerning tastes.

As residents of an international port, the people of Louisbourg had access to a wider variety of food than their counterparts in the land-locked villages of Europe. All except the poorest people enjoyed the luxury of freshly ground coffee and sugar, shipped in from the Caribbean. Cream was a less plentiful commodity, available only to residents who kept a cow (or, more likely, a goat) tethered in the backyard. Most livestock arrived "on the hoof," aboard ships travelling from Acadia or New England. By 1728, free-ranging pigs were so abundant that local authorities forced residents to pen them.

France led the fashion in food, as it did in many other things. By the 18th century, cooks no longer relied on cloves and pepper to disguise the flavour of spoiled meat. Instead, they chose high-quality ingredients, delicately enhanced by the temperate use of herbs and spices. Louisbourg's kitchen gardens yielded numerous herbs including parsley, chives, basil and thyme. When meat was scarce, their turnips, carrots and beans helped fill out a soup or stew. Dried peas from Quebec also provided extra calories. Potatoes would have served admirably in this capacity, but people still looked upon them with disfavour. Instead, people filled up on bread. Jean Seigneur's guests dined on white bread. Next door, at the Hôtel de la Marine, soldiers and fishers were content with the dark heavy bread of the working classes.

Neither group would have turned up their noses at a dish of kidneys, tongue or oxtail. With livestock so difficult to obtain, nothing was wasted. Pigs provided such delicacies as pigs' feet, while their intestines and other organs were converted into sausages. The poultry of Louisbourg in no way resembled our own fat chickens. Slightly stringy from an active life in the barnyard, chickens were killed only when they ceased to produce eggs.

In addition to domestic animals, the townspeople consumed small game such as rabbit, squirrel and partridge. They shot migrating birds that flew overhead and stalked resting fowl in the long grasses outside the fortress walls. Young boys with a few rabbits strung to their belts probably showed up on the Seigneur's doorstep frequently, hoping to sell their prizes to the innkeeper. By far the most readily available form of protein was Louisbourg's own salted codfish. As Roman Catholics, the townspeople were forbidden to eat meat on Fridays and Saturdays. The entire 40 days of Lent were also meatless. French cooks had a wealth of recipes dedicated to the preparation of cod.

The weeks leading up to Lent, known as Carnival, gave townspeople an opportunity to indulge their physical appetites. The upper classes celebrated with intimate suppers and evenings of cards. In the governor's apartments, dozens of candles kept out the cold winter night as guests danced and feasted on potted meats, brandied fruit and other delicacies shipped from France. The lower classes celebrated in taverns, with plenty of rum and wine. Since Louisbourg residents could not marry during Lent, weddings were another reason for celebration. The festivities culminated in Mardi Gras, or Shrove Tuesday. The next morning, Ash Wednesday, saw the townspeople rise

bright and early for mass. The town remained fairly quiet until late spring, when the first ships arrived from France. At that time, much of the activity centred on taverns such as the Hôtel de la Marine, which was often the first stop for sailors and fishers. Workers from nearby construction sites also nipped in for a quick drink.

Today, visitors dine in atmospheres similar to those that greeted the inns' 18th-century patrons. Park staff have furnished À l'Épée Royale according to an inventory made at the time of Jean Seigneur's death. In its refined atmosphere, diners can expect to find a full setting of cutlery. In the more rustic Hôtel de la Marine and Grandchamp Inn, diners receive only a large spoon. The 18th-century patrons of working class inns rarely, if ever, enjoyed the luxury of a fork.

À l'Épée Royale takes a break in the sunshine.

Top: Hôtel de la Marine

Bottom: Server at À l'Épée Royale takes a break in the sunshine.

In all three restaurants, dishes are prepared according to the original recipes, using the same ingredients available in the 18th century. Menu selections include meat, fish, soup, salad, rice, pasta, vegetables, dessert, and beverages. A children's menu is also available.

PROFILE: LOUISE THÉRÈSE PETIT

People fortunate enough to acquire property along the quay often opened their homes to paying guests. A spruce bough over the door let people know they served alcoholic beverages. This was the case with Louise Thérèse Petit and her husband, retired soldier Julien Auger dit Grandchamp. The couple lived in their small house next door to the Hôtel de la Marine and ran their adjoining property as an inn. For Julien and Louise Thérèse, the inn was an insurance against their old age.

On Julien Auger's death in 1741, Louise Thérèse assumed full control of the inn. As their husband's inheritors, widows

Left: A lady and her maid in the home of the commissaire-ordonnateur

Below: Grandchamps Inn

often controlled the family business, holding it in trust to divide with adult children. Since children did not reach their majority until the age of 25 (for females) or 30 (for males), these women often enjoyed a long, unchallenged reign. They were free to sign contracts, buy property and negotiate their children's marriages.

Louise Thérèse Petit was fortunate indeed to enjoy such a marked degree of independence. In contrast, military wives were often forced to remarry quickly or eke out a living from a small pension. The widows of labourers took in washing or hired out themselves, and their children, as servants. Servants comprised 15 percent of Louisbourg's total population in 1737. Louise Thérèse Petit would have relied on servants and a slave to help in the day-to-day operation of her inn.

For a family living on the edge, it was easy to fall into servitude. Some children were contracted out when they were as young as seven years of age. Often, the parent or guardian of the child entered into a contract with the employer, setting the wages (if any) and the terms of service. Most servants were single and lived in the houses of their employers. Some, such as the governor's valet and steward (maître d'hôtel), were professionals with strictly defined functions. However, most servants found life an unending round of routine jobs. A female servant busied herself in the kitchen and the yard, in lighting fires, cooking, washing clothes and gardening. Male servants were often responsible for the animals, wood-chopping, cleaning shoes and running errands. Servants ate apart from their employers, and slept on pallets in the kitchen or stables, depending on their place of work.

Servants were encouraged to remember their place. One Louisbourg court case involved the daughter of a merchant. Her father claimed she had been treated as a servant by the family with which she boarded. In Louisbourg's hierarchical society, the taint of servitude was sufficiently damning for the father to defend his daughter's status in court.

Top: Washing up is a job common to any century.
Bottom: Polishing pewter

51

FRÉDÉRIC GATE & DESTOUCHES HOUSE

Guests at the Grandchamps Inn had front row seats to the whole panorama of life in Louisbourg. Sooner or later, everyone in Louisbourg showed up at the Frédéric Gate, which was located just in front of the inn. Residents strolled down to the quay to hear the sailors' harrowing tales of a difficult crossing or the lucky escape from an English privateer. Men of the merchant marine doubtless enlightened the townspeople about life on the coast of Africa and the strange creatures they encountered there. Children listened to the mix of accents and gaped at the various regional costumes.

As passengers disembarked, dock workers unloaded goods destined for the king's warehouse, located on the quay in front of the Frédéric Gate. Soldiers manned the sentry box outside the warehouse and stood guard over valuable cargo on the king's vessels. Representatives from the Admiralty Court were busy registering new arrivals, checking for illicit goods, and controlling the traffic in the harbour. The

Admiralty was also responsible for investigating shipwrecks. One day in August, 1725, word reached Louisbourg that the King's vessel *Chameau* had gone down under full sail during a wild storm the night before, with 310 souls aboard. Search parties were quickly organized to identify the victims and recover the chest of gold and silver coins sent out to pay the soldiers. Some of the dead, including the new *intendant* of New France and the son of the governor of Montreal, were soon recovered and buried in the small fishing village of Baleine. The wreck itself was not found until 1965.

Much of the town's official life went on near the Frédéric Gate. Marine drummers, in blue coats liberally decorated with red and white braid, drew a crowd as an official read out the latest ordinance or announced an upcoming auction. Auctions were often held right there on the quay, with the goods clearly laid out for the bidders' viewing. Goods ranged from a load of ship's gear to the clothing of a dead relative. Crowds also gathered in

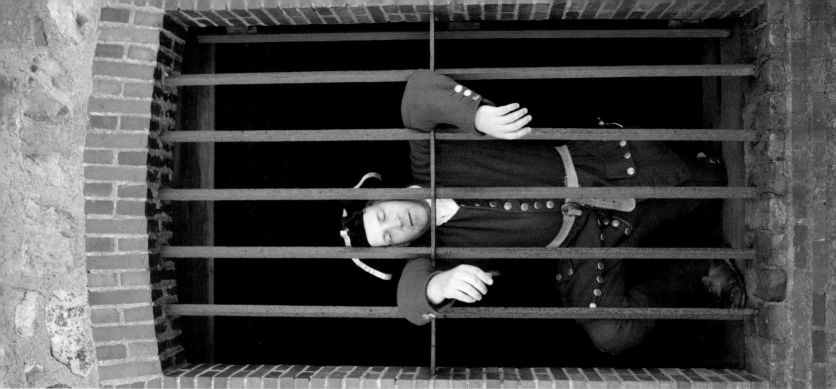

front of the *carcan* (pillory), located just beyond the Frédéric Gate. No doubt the accused and the townspeople traded insults.

The Destouches house and bakery, located next door to the Grandchamps Inn, was another busy shop on the Louisbourg quay. It supplied bread to the civilian population of Louisbourg. Some people preferred to pay a small charge and bake their own dough in the large ovens.

Master baker Nicolas Pugnant dit Destouches profited from his position at the top of his craft. His fine house was built to replace an older, *piquet* structure that had burnt down in 1737. By 1744, his widow Marie Brunet probably lived alone here with her 21-year-old son, her other children having either died or married. Visitors can purchase light refreshments at the Destouches House, which is run as a coffee shop by the Fortress Louisbourg Association.

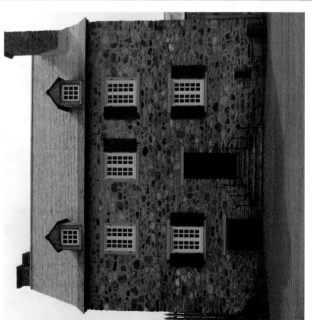

Opposite page: Townspeople at the Frédéric Gate
Right: A soldier of the Karrer regiment loiters in the king's warehouse.
Below: Destouches home and bakery

COMMISSAIRE-ORDONNATEUR RESIDENCE

Next door, the official residence of the *commissaire-ordonnateur* occupies three town lots. The toothed stones at the waterside end of the building allowed for expansion, or for the construction of a neighbouring building if required. Unfortunately, fate decreed otherwise.

This building was the administrative and financial centre of Ile Royale. Here, the *commissaire-ordonnateur* received the royal ordinances and had them copied, to post at strategic points in the town. All civil, judicial and financial records were also archived here. A corps of clerks organized the colony's census records, ministerial correspondence, and statistics on the amount of fish caught and exported. The Royal Treasury was located on the lower floor.

Among Louisbourg's five *commissaire-ordonnateurs*, François Bigot was the most famous, and the most colourful. As a young bureaucrat, Bigot had risen slowly but steadily through the ranks at the *Ministère de la Marine*. His posting to Louisbourg in 1739 was a step closer to his ultimate goal: a posting as *intendant* in one of the ports of France. With this in mind, he threw himself into his new duties, with mixed success.

One of Bigot's primary objectives was to stimulate the development of new industry. Although Ile Royale had rich seams of coal, Bigot could not find a buyer in France. He had somewhat more success with shipbuilding. In the end, however, Louisbourg entrepreneurs preferred to purchase English ships loaded with supplies, paying for them with rum and molasses from the West Indies.

Bigot was more successful in supplying the fortress with food. Unfortunately, this brought him head-to-head with authorities in France. Throughout the 18th century,

Left: Clerk in an office in the commissaire-ordonnateur's residence

Opposite page: Citizens lived and died according to the king's decree.

Europe firmly adhered to the mercantilist theory of commerce. Baldly stated, this meant that French colonies existed to supply the mother country with raw materials, while consuming French surplus and manufactured goods.

Economists argued that, by turning to New England for supplies, Louisbourg enriched the English colonies at the expense of France. Bigot, concerned with the immediate problem of feeding a population at low cost, gave little thought to the finer points of economic theory. He continued to buy grain from the English colonies, right up until the eve of war. In 1743, 78 ships from mainland Nova Scotia and New England brought goods to replenish Louisbourg's stores. Careful rationing saw the populace through the next two years of war. At the end of the siege, there was still merchandise in the storehouse. The ever-practical Bigot sold it to the English.

Bigot devoted equal thought to the administration of his private fortune. When France and Great Britain went to war in 1744, Bigot bought shares in three privateer vessels. Certainly, he had no scruples about plundering the ships of Louisbourg's erstwhile trading partners, the New England-ers. Both he and Governor du Quesnel held shares in the *Cantabre*, which was captured off Cape Cod in 1744.

Bigot went on to fame (or infamy) as the last *Intendant* of New France. He arrived in Quebec in 1748 and remained until the colony's capitulation in 1760. The intervening years were spent in a brilliant and frenzied social life, where his gambling became legendary. Entertaining was actually part of Bigot's job description, though perhaps it did not require quite the amount of zeal that he brought to the task. In both Louisbourg and Quebec, Bigot was the centre of a complicated network of patronage. Influential builders frequented the *soirées* of the *commissaire-ordonnateur*, hoping to win government tenders.

In French society, anyone aspiring to move in these circles had to follow strict, if unwritten, codes of behaviour. These standards were set in Versailles and extended to posture, conversation, dancing, and music. Most upper-class men and women had received enough musical training as children to be able to perform capably at private parties. In the 18th century, the harpsichord and the baroque guitar were the instruments of choice for many

ladies, while gentleman often played the flute or violin. Even in Louisbourg, the upper classes enjoyed a high standard of musical entertainment. In the garrisons, professional musicians were recruited into the military with the express purpose of providing the officers with musical entertainment. In Louisbourg, one of the most gifted of these was 14-year old Christophe Chiquelier, Jr., son of the Keeper of the King's Instruments in France.

Dancing was another important social skill. In Louisbourg, upper-class children, both boys and girls, studied with dancing masters to perfect the turn of a leg or the proper execution of a pirouette. Among the lower classes, dancing was more exuberant. With men far outnumbering women, most dancing probably consisted of a fisherman jumping up to execute the folk dances of his native province or grabbing the innkeeper's wife for an impromptu turn on the floor. This was accomplished to the music of flute, whistle, fiddle, or hurdy-gurdy.

Left: Detail on desk

Below: A hurdy-gurdy provides a source of light entertainment for society's lower strata.

View from a French Warship *by artist Lewis Parker*

LOUISBOURG AS A NAVAL PORT

The second floor of the *commissaire-ordonnateur's* residence contains visitor's washrooms located to the right of the stairway. To your left is an exhibit featuring reminders of Louisbourg's vital connection with the sea, as well as original objects from the colonial town.

Since the maritime theme is difficult to illustrate, Canadian artist Lewis Parker was commissioned to prepare two large paintings on the theme. One painting, entitled *View from the Clock Tower* (page 19) offers a panoramic view of the harbour as it would have appeared in the summer of 1744. The painting entitled *View from a French Warship* portrays the activities on the quay.

Parker accepted the assignment in 1981 and completed it 16 months later. Fully 70 percent of his time was spent in research. For the first painting, park staff gathered information on the ships actually in the harbour on August 18, 1744. Parker also worked from isometric drawings of actual 18th-century buildings. Among the most compelling parts of the murals are the scenarios of moments in 18th-century life: the soldiers cutting firewood, the servant with the basket of fresh vegetables, the children fishing. In *View from the Clock Tower*, Captain de Gannes is pictured in front of his house, talking to a servant. Pierre-Paul d'Espiet de la Plagne and his wife Marie Charlotte deLort appear on the balcony of their house.

LE BILLARD TAVERN

The large house across the street from the property of the *commissaire-ordonnateur* was the home of one of Louisbourg's surgeons. It is not open to the public. The adjacent empty lot (marked with a large cross) was intended for the parish church; that church, however, was never built. Louisbourg's thrifty townspeople were content to worship in the small military chapel.

Farther along the quay, next door to the surgeon's house, a small tavern known as "Le Billard" was run by another enterprising woman, the Widow Beauséjour. This cabaret housed one of at least 14 billiard tables in the town. Most innkeepers provided their guests with some form of entertainment. Playing cards were an important export product in France, and hundreds of decks arrived in Louisbourg each year. In 1741, Julien Auger dit Grandchamp had 30 decks of cards in his establishment.

Cards and rum can be an explosive combination. To prevent the violence that often followed heavy losses, certain games were banned. A litany of names made up the forbidden list: *bassette, pharaon, lansquenet, boca, quinquenoue, barbacole* and *berlitry.* In most of these games,

Above: Le Billard Tavern
Below: Few could resist the lure of the town's gaming tables.

At Le Billard, pewter reflected the landlady's growing prosperity.

players bet on the layout of the cards as they were dealt. Innkeepers were forbidden to let people play illegal games on the premises. In Louisbourg, however, gambling was a way of life—too firmly entrenched to be stopped by a mere law. People bet on the turn of a card and the spill of the dice. Catherine Auger, the innkeeper's married daughter, once took a ship's pilot to court for failing to pay up. The bet? The outcome of her pregnancy. The wager? A pair of shoes.

The upper classes did not feel pressured to set a good example. *Commissaire-ordonnateur* Bigot's growing obsession with gambling would eventually earn him a reprimand from his superiors. When he was *Intendant* of New France, he once lost 204,000 *livres* at the forbidden game of *faro*. The authorities were also not above using gam-

bling for their own purposes. Official lotteries, offering substantial cash prizes, helped enrich government coffers. At the same time, authorities frowned on the smaller lotteries that were always being organized by small, independent promoters. People regularly bought cheap tickets on small prizes—perhaps a bottle of imported brandy or a second-hand suit. The lower classes also enjoyed lotto, a game similar to bingo.

With the occasional exception of Le Billard, the houses on this block are not open to the public. Instead, they house fire-fighting equipment (including a fire truck), the costume department, work areas and building materials. Take a few moments to examine the various architectural styles and construction methods of the reconstructed houses, then proceed to the harbour wall.

LIGHTHOUSE POINT & LOUISBOURG RUINS

Hospital ruins in the foreground

In the 18th century, the far shore was nearly as busy as the quay itself. At the careening wharf, ships damaged in the crossing were turned on their side, to have their planks repaired and tarred. While Louisbourg slept, the lighthouse keeper on the point kept his lantern blazing, their light a welcome signal to ships approaching the coast. The original lighthouse, built in 1733, was the first in Canada, and the second in North America, after Boston. Its beam shone 29 km (18 miles) out to sea.

The lighthouse point played a strategic role in both sieges. The Island Battery, a fortification situated on the nearest island, lay only 923 metres (1000 yards) across the channel. This battery was one of two main defenses trained on the harbour, the expected site of attack. In the first siege of 1745, the French abandoned the Royal Battery early on, leaving the Island Battery to defend the harbour.

This siege promised no glorious naval victory for Commodore Warren and the British ships of the line. Their sole encounter was with the *Vigilant*, one of two ships sent from France to protect the fortress. This lone ship, carrying needed ammunition and supplies, was easily captured after a short chase. The British ships once again settled down to wait.

Consider the attackers' dilemma: the New England artillery slowly pounding down the walls would, in time, force a breach. However, the infantry would suffer heavy losses as they stormed through the wall in the face of French fire. From the attackers' point of view, it was far better to force a quick surrender by having the ships enter the harbour, guns blazing.

At first, boatloads of New Englanders tried to take the Island Battery in an amphibious assault, with heavy losses. They soon realized it was far easier to set up gun batteries on Lighthouse Point. They hauled their cannon around the harbour and overpowered the battery within days. The French, realizing the peril of a frontal naval attack, surrendered.

British commanders successfully copied this same strategy early in the siege of 1758, marching their divisions around the harbour to the point. Although the French had taken the precaution of setting up a gun post in the area, they knew they could not hold it against the British troops. They abandoned the post and escaped to the fortress. The British immediately opened fire on the island. By mid-June, the Island Battery was silenced.

Meanwhile, the British had set up gun batteries all along the harbour. From Lighthouse Point to the Dauphin Gate, the French found themselves facing a ring of fire. Still,

the British pressed on. By June 16, they had established a battery just beyond the King's Bastion. Cannon balls destroyed the chapel and the soldiers' barracks, while hardly a house in town escaped. The French accused the British of concentrating on civilian targets. Even the hospital was hit, and the surgeon killed.

As the land battle raged, five French men-of-war and a frigate were trapped in the harbour by the British ships circling just outside. The French naval commanders have been criticized for retreating from the British gun batteries until they were under the very walls of the fortress. This had the effect of drawing enemy fire ever closer to the town itself, where cannonballs meant for the French ships crashed into the roofs of the houses.

Only the frigate *Aréthuse* mounted an aggressive assault. In the end, she slipped through the British defenses, carrying news of the fortress' predicament to France. The other ships were either burnt, sunk, or captured; the *Bienfaisant* was put into the service of the British. The people of Louisbourg were shipped out shortly after, and the fortifications destroyed. Today, the remains of the *Célèbre*, the *Capricieux*, the *Prudent* and the *Entreprenant* lie at the bottom of Louisbourg Harbour. For most of the intervening centuries, the site lay forgotten to the world.

A WALK THROUGH THE RUINS

Beyond the last block lie the original ruins of Louisbourg. These windswept meadows, which represent three-quarters of the town, were once crowded with homes, warehouses, boutiques and workshops. Today, the area is an important archaeological site, protected by the Government of Canada. An interesting reconstructed feature just outside the ruins area is the sluice gate, designed to raise and lower the level of water in the pond. It is a fine example of 18th-century technology. To reach it, take the path leading from the houses to the reconstructed guardhouse. From there, you can follow the beach to the far point. Visitors who prefer a shorter walk can retrace their steps from the houses, walking towards the old museum. A dirt road to your left leads to the ruins, which are clearly marked with interpretive panels.

The Louisbourg tour ends at the old museum, built in 1936 to commemorate the role Louisbourg played in the history of North America. Today, it remains as a tribute to all the people who worked so hard to see the Old Town reborn.

Ironically, the people who served as catalysts for Louisbourg's rebirth came from New England, the land that once hastened its destruction. In 1895, the Society of Colonial Wars, based in New York, proposed to erect a monument to the New England war dead. The Acadian senator and author Pascal Poirier was incensed at what he saw as a celebration of Louisbourg's defeat and destruction. Although the ceremony went ahead as planned, Pascal Poirier continued to speak out on behalf of Louisbourg. He also lent his name to the Louisbourg Memorial Fund, established in 1903 by Captain D.J. Kennelly, manager of the Sydney and Louisbourg Coal and Railway Company. Its patrons included King Edward VII of England, Sir Charles Tupper, and Robert Borden.

Unfortunately, official interest in the site died with Kennelly and Poirier. It would take another coal company man to kindle it again. J.S. McLennan arrived in Cape Breton on behalf of the International Coal Company and remained as the publisher of the Sydney Post. McLennan's book, entitled *Louisbourg: From its Foundation to its Fall*, was published in 1918 and remains a comprehensive work on the fortress and the sieges. At the time of

Top: A woodworker's light touch
Bottom: Original museum, opened in 1936

McLennan's involvement, the Louisbourg site was carved up into 20 privately-owned lots. Thanks to intense lobbying on McLennan's part, the Parks Branch of the Department of the Interior purchased two of these lots in 1921. In 1926, the federal government declared the site to be an historic place. One of its earliest visitors was the Quebec nationalist and journalist Henri Bourassa, who took up the cause in the Canadian House of Commons.

By 1928, most of the property was in the hands of the government and Louisbourg was declared a National Historic Site. The present masonry museum opened in 1936, with Katharine McLennan, the Senator's daughter, as Honorary Curator. Her model of the town has stood the test of time and new research. It continues to fascinate visitors today.

THE 1960 INITIATIVE

The impetus to reconstruct Louisbourg grew out of the socio-economic conditions prevailing in Cape Breton in the mid-20th century. By 1960, the island was facing one of the greatest crises in its history: the closure of its coal mines. Along with steel, coal represented one of the area's two major industries. Now, hydro-electric power, natural gas, and petroleum were beginning to eclipse coal on the world markets.

As the coal mines began to close, hundreds of people faced the loss of their livelihood. In 1960, the federal government stepped in. A royal commission chaired by the Honourable I.C. Rand recommended the reconstruction of the Fortress of Louisbourg as a way to diversify the island economy. Prime Minister Diefenbaker, himself a passionate student of history, applauded the idea.

In the years that followed, approximately 225 former coal miners were trained as stonemasons, bricklayers and carpenters. Others found work as labourers. After almost 250 years, the walls of Louisbourg began to rise again. When the construction was completed, many miners used their newly acquired skills in other sectors of the economy.

Basket weaving

A soldier on the ramparts

AN ARCHAEOLOGICAL TREASURE

Although the British military blew up Louisbourg's town walls in 1760, the homes and warehouses, streets and gardens remained. Over the next 25 years, most fell into ruin while others were mined for their brick and cut stone. After Sydney became the capital of the new colony of Cape Breton in 1785, Louisbourg was left to a handful of Irish farmers and fishers. Their gardens and livestock did little to disturb the encroaching grass and sod. Unlike the colonial towns of Boston, New York, Philadelphia, New Orleans and Quebec, Louisbourg's landscape remained free of skyscrapers, railway tracks and freeways. What remained was an archaeological treasure.

Once excavation began, each area targeted for reconstruction was carefully laid out on a grid. Archaeologists meticulously recorded the location of building ruins, fortifications, streets, drains and garbage heaps. Luckily, the boggy, acid soils of Louisbourg helped to preserve leather

and wool. Archaeologists encountered shoes, buckles and wooden buckets. To date, only five percent of the total site has been excavated. In all, about five million artifacts have been recovered and the majority have been stored in accessible, climate-controlled environments. Each artifact tells a story. Pieces of Chinese porcelain in a garbage dump reveal much about trade links. A toy boat yields important clues about the nature of family life.

The archaeological record is supported and reinforced by an equally impressive body of historical data. Fortress historians combed archives in North America and Europe for documentation relating to the 18th-century colony. The result is over 750,000 pages of documents (mostly copies of correspondence maintained by the 18th-century government officials in the town).

Over 500 maps and plans provided a starting point for the reconstruction. A property plan drawn up in 1734 showed every lot in town, while detailed plans also existed for public buildings. (Archaeologists sometimes discovered that not all public buildings were constructed strictly to plan. In fact, several different plans often existed for the same building. For the right side of the Dauphin Demi-Bastion, there were 19 possibilities to choose from.) Unfortunately, there were few existing plans for private homes. The fortress interpretive team relied on archaeologists to reveal the locations of chimneys and doorways, as well as privies, sheds and other outbuildings. Estate inventories revealed the number of rooms and their contents. Court records might describe the backyard where a crime took place, or refer to a wall. Where no information was available on a specific building, members of the interpretive team used their own knowledge of 18th-century building techniques to provide the necessary detail.

The fortress interpretive team chose the year 1744 as its focus. By then, the fortifications were nearly complete and the town had reached its full potential as a fishing and trading centre. It was also a year before the destruction caused by the siege of 1745.

As you tour the site, you will notice that some of the most important buildings such as the hospital, the convent

Reading an estate inventory

school, the Admiralty Court and the Maurepas Gate have not been reconstructed. Although these buildings would undoubtedly illuminate Louisbourg's institutional life, they would also have been separated from each other by wide spaces and ruins (budgetary restraints prohibited the reconstruction of the entire town). Instead, the fortress interpretive team chose to reconstruct one complete quarter of the town area, from the fortification walls to the waterfront. Crowded with homes, taverns and gardens, this quarter conveys a sense of daily life in Louisbourg. The area's quay and government buildings represent the town's official life, while the King's Bastion and the Dauphin Bastion indicate a military presence.

The artifacts on site fall into three categories: those that can be traced to 18th-century Louisbourg or were excavated on site; 18th-century objects which have no direct link to Louisbourg; and reproductions. Foremost among them are the artifacts which belonged to the people of Louisbourg. The upper floors of the soldiers' barracks feature an exhibit of the archaeological objects excavated on site. Other artifacts travelled a long and circuitous route back to Louisbourg. These are displayed in the house of the *commissaire-ordonnateur*. The painting of Rochefort in this exhibit was believed to have been taken from Louisbourg by William Pepperrell, commander of the land forces during the first siege. A silver chalice is reputed to have been used by the priest and missionary to the Mi'kmaq, Abbé Maillard.

Of all the objects in this class, the Louisbourg Cross has taken the longest time to return. Legend has it that the New England soldiers claimed it as booty after the siege of 1745. It ended up at Harvard University, where it survived both fire and vandalism. For most of the 20th century, it adorned one of the entrances to the Harvard University Library. The cross was finally returned to Louisbourg in 1995, during the celebration of the 250th anniversary of the first siege. Representatives from Harvard accompanied the cross to Cape Breton.

Other objects of note on the site have no direct association with Louisbourg. Many of these were acquired

by Jean Palardy, a dealer and collector of 18th-century French furniture. When compiling the collection, Palardy

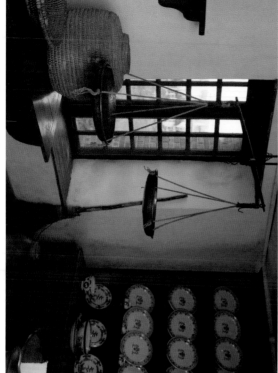

In the governor's pantry, sausages provided a solution to the lack of refrigeration.

was provided with acquisition lists compiled from estate inventories. Many of his most valuable acquisitions are displayed in the governor's apartments.

Louisbourg was established during the reign of Louis XIV and destroyed during the reign of Louis XV. Accordingly, the furniture collection contains samples from both reigns, with a slight emphasis on the earlier pieces. Since Louisbourg's settlers would have brought along some of their older furniture, park curators have included some Louis XIII pieces in the collection.

Approximately half of the items on display in the furnished buildings are period reproductions. Small iron fragments of door hinges and other pieces excavated on site served as models for the reconstruction. Pewtersmiths crafted the cutlery used in the period kitchens and restaurants, while carpenters produced the hand-carved armoires. The earthenware pots and ceramic dishes were made by using the same processes as 18th-century potters. If you look closely, you may see the potter's fingerprints on a piece.

HISTORICAL ACCURACY

Throughout the reconstruction, park staff continually found it necessary to balance their goal of accuracy with the need to meet modern standards of comfort, health, and safety. Original foundations were often used in the reconstruction. Safety concerns, however, sometimes made it necessary to reinforce the foundations, or rebuild them entirely, using selected original stones. In all, six buildings were built on their original foundations: the King's Bastion guardhouse, the barracks, the ice-house, the Dauphin Demi-Bastion, the powder magazine, and the engineer's residence. Other reconstructions often incorporated original stones, bits of a drain, or part of the floor. All, with the exception of the fishing property, are built in their original locations.

Since 18th-century standards of warmth and comfort fall far below our own, the final design also had to include modern washrooms, heated rooms, and comfortable seating. For preservation purposes, valuable artifacts had to be displayed in conditions of controlled lighting and temperature. Park staff rose to the challenge. Water lines and electricity were installed out of visual range, without disturbing valuable archaeological sites. To preserve the ambiance on site, all lounges and display areas incorporate 18th-century materials or design elements into their construction and decor.

The same attention to detail extends to every department. Although the food served in Louisbourg kitchens is based on 18th-century recipes, it is prepared with meticulous attention to modern health standards. The costumes of the animators are made to be as accurate as possible. Costume staff researched 18th-century paintings, Diderot's *Encyclopédie*, and the descriptions of clothing found in estate inventories. Original 18th-century clothes were also used as models. Archaeological excavations yielded buttons, which were copied. All costumes are made from natural materials such as silk, linen, wool, leather and cotton.

Unfortunately, costume staff do not always have access to the same variety of design and quality of fabric available to 18th-century consumers. With the advent of synthetic fibres, certain weaves and brocades have become increasingly hard to find.

As time goes on, park staff is continually challenged to find new ways of interpreting the history of Louisbourg. Children's interpretive programs help young visitors explore themes of 18th-century life while their parents pursue their own interests. Every August, staff and visitors celebrate the *Fête de Saint-Louis* just as the original residents of Louisbourg did, with garden parties, dancing, and a *Te Deum* sung in the chapel.

In 1995, the fortress hosted the Grand Encampment, 250 years after the first siege and 275 years after Louisbourg was named the capital of Ile Royale. That summer, over 1200 historical reenactors from all over North America recreated an 18th-century military camp. Earlier, in 1993, the Disney movie *Squanto: A Warrior's Tale* was filmed on site. Couples have chosen to celebrate their marriages in the 18th-century chapel, while diving enthusiasts follow local guides on an underwater tour of the harbour. The opportunities to enjoy the Fortress of Louisbourg are as diverse as the people who visit the site.

BACK TO THE BUSES

From the former Louisbourg museum, you have a host of options: enjoy a glass of wine or a bowl of hot soup at the Grandchamps Inn; read a few chapters from one of the books in the theme lounges; strike up a conversation with a young soldier from the *Compagnies franches de la Marine*. To find the buses, retrace your steps back to the Dauphin Gate and the fishing property beyond. The buses leave every 10 to 15 minutes.

Authenticity is key for Louisbourg's costume staff.

NATURE ACTIVITIES AND HERITAGE TRAILS

The Louisbourg National Historic Site extends over an area of more than 6,700 hectares (16,550 acres). Within the park, there are several nature walks with an historical focus.

MI'KMAQ TRAIL

The Mi'kmaq trail, located just across from the Visitor Reception Centre, is marked by a series of interpretive panels that explore the role of the Mi'kmaq people in the history of Louisbourg. This trail affords a spectacular view of the harbour, the lighthouse point, and the site of the old Island Battery (no longer existing). It is the same view that greeted the New England troops as they emerged from the woods and began to plan their strategy for taking the fortress. Total walking time is approximately 15 minutes.

ROYAL BATTERY SITE

One of the New Englanders' first military targets was the Royal Battery, originally located just below the site of the modern Visitor Reception Centre. After leaving the Visitor Reception Centre, turn right at the gate onto the main road. Follow the signs to the site of the Royal Battery.

SIMON POINT TRAIL

Another nature walk follows the line of Freshwater Brook, the site of the attackers' camps in both sieges. To locate this trail, leave the Visitor Reception Centre and follow the paved road back to the town of Louisbourg. Turn left at the fountain and continue up the hill. The pavement gives way to a graded road as you follow the signs to Kennington Cove. The Simon Point trail lies just beyond the small shelter on the far side of the brook. Park your car on the side of the road and follow the wide path to the sea. Total walking time is approximately 20 minutes.

A fountain in the modern town of Louisbourg recalls the area's historic past.

Top: Simon Point Trail

Middle: A bridge on the Simon Point Trail offers a refreshing aspect.

Above: Kennington Cove

KENNINGTON COVE BEACH

Another 3 km (2 miles) past this trail lies the beach where, w during the second siege, the attackers landed men and guns before proceeding overland to Louisbourg. Today, the sandy beach and well-groomed picnic grounds belie the area's violent past. Near the fortress itself, on the Kennington Cove Road, the Marconi Picnic Area recalls the work of Guglielmo Marconi. This Italian inventor sent the first transatlantic wireless message from towers located in Table Head, Glace Bay. A receiving station was once located here.

LIGHTHOUSE POINT

From the town fountain, another option is to circle the harbour past the towr to Lighthouse Point. Interpretive panels explore the role it played in both sieges. Another series of panels near the lighthouse describes the history of the light. The light you see today was constructed in 1923–24.

SIEGE CAMP TOUR

The Siege Camp Tcur is a 2-km (1.5-mi) walking tour, self-guided with handheld GPS, through the hills surrounding the fortress, where British military camps were set up in 1758 as 15,000 troops prepared to lay siege. A series of interpretive panels will be situated at key points of interest along the way. For 2010 the trail is partially open with temporary interpretation (site markers and brochure).

WOLFE'S REDOUBT

The Wolfe's Redoubt Trail is a fully-accessible 200-m (220-yd) path through woods to a defensive earthenwork called a redoubt (a small fort), constructed by British soldiers under Brigadier General James Wolfe during the siege of Louisbourg in 1758. The redoubt is situated across from the exit of Parking Lot 5. The trail has interpretive panels, two mid-route rest areas, and a viewing deck with benches.

TOWN OF LOUISBOURG

Main Street in the modern town of Louisbourg

After the British systematically blew up the fortifications of Louisbourg, the area was colonized by retired soldiers of the British regiments and some merchants who had served in the British garrison. Gradually the population shifted its base to the other side of the harbour, in an area they referred to as the New Town, or "Louisbourg."

After the American Revolution, 40 United Empire Loyalists arrived to join the people settled in Louisbourg. After a single winter, however, the lack of firewood and general poverty of the area forced them to move to Sydney, where they joined the Loyalists organized by J.F.W. DesBarres.

For many years, the people who remained in Louisbourg continued to live as people had always lived along these shores—by fishing. Later, with the development of Cape Breton's mining industry, Louisbourg once more became a trans-shipment point. This time, the resource was coal, not cod.

The first mines had been opened by the French in 1720, in Cow Bay (known today as Port Morien). By the end of the 19th century, there were 30 new mines in Cape Breton, centered mainly in Glace Bay, New Waterford and Sydney Mines. Since Louisbourg's ice-free harbour permitted year-round shipping, it was chosen as a central depot. In 1891 the Dominion Coal Company assumed ownership of several private coal mines and provided the impetus and capital to link all the small railways servicing the mines. Coal was sent to Louisbourg on the S & L (Sydney and Louisbourg) Railway, incorporated in 1894. From Louisbourg, the coal was shipped to Britain.

The town continued to prosper. During World Wars I and II, the coal and steel industries were vital to the war effort. After 200 years, convoys of ships gathered once more in Louisbourg Harbour, in readiness for the dangerous passage across the Atlantic.

Those days are over. The S & L Railway was another victim of the closing of the Cape Breton coal mines in the 1960s. Even the fisheries, which sustained the town for so many centuries, are now in doubt. The people, however, remain resilient through hard times. Today, the residents of Louisbourg (as it is now spelled) are presiding over new growth in tourism and culture.

GETTING TO LOUISBOURG

Louisbourg is the shire town of District 1, in the Cape Breton Regional Municipality. Driving time from Sydney is approximately 30 minutes (34 km/21 miles) on Route 22. Visitors can also approach the town from Glace Bay, via the Marconi Trail on Route 25 (51 km/32 miles).

MAIN STREET

Louisbourg's main street is lined with grocery and hardware stores, a liquor store and gift shops. Visitor services include a bank, medical clinic, Tourism Cape Breton Information Centre and auto repair facilities. The town is served by five churches and a public library.

THE HARBOUR

The harbour remains the focal point of the town. On its recreational boardwalk are a signal mast and interpretive panels outlining Louisbourg's history, from prehistoric times to the present.

ACCOMMODATIONS & ATTRACTIONS

The town's accommodations include a motel, several luxury inns, motor home parks, a recreational vehicle park and campground, housekeeping cottages and several bed-and-breakfast facilities. Local restaurants offer a variety of freshly landed seafood, including lobster, scallops, halibut and cod. In August, the town hosts Nova Scotia's only Crab Festival, with a menu featuring snow crab, fresh mussels, potato salad, cole slaw and dessert accompanied by tea and coffee. Local entertainers offer a taste of the island's musical heritage.

S & L RAILWAY MUSEUM

The S & L Railway Museum, located at the entrance to modern Louisbourg, interprets the history of the town's boom years at the turn of the 20th century. From June to September, visitors can climb aboard a restored train and visit the station master's home and office. The original station contains an exhibit of railroad memorabilia and the Samuel Clarke collection of watercolours.

Nearby, the freight shed houses an electric scale model of the S & L Railway, the pier and the freight wharf. At the newly constructed Roundhouse, visitors and townspeople enjoy summer dances, ceilidhs, concerts, teas and other community events. The Roundhouse's exhibit of antique and modern memorial quilts is one of the finest anywhere.

LOUISBOURG PLAYHOUSE

The Louisbourg Playhouse was originally constructed

S & L Railway Museum

at the Fortress of Louisbourg as part of the set for the movie *Squanto: A Warrior's Tale*. In 1993, the Louisbourg District Planning and Development Commission moved the building to its present location on Aberdeen Street. Today, the Louisbourg Playhouse Society operates it as a centre for the performing arts and offers nightly entertainment during the summer. As always, the people of Louisbourg look to the future, even as they keep their past, their culture and their heritage vibrant and alive.

For the student of history, Louisbourg has much to offer. The drama of its past and the existence of original documents has long made it a focus for research and discovery. One of the earliest and most famous studies of the town is J.S. McLennan's *Louisbourg: From its Foundation to its Fall*, published in 1918. Based on documents found in the National Archives of France, it explores Louisbourg's role in the French-English struggle for empire. It also provides a detailed analysis of the two sieges and the relative strengths of the opposing forces.

The reference section of your local library is another excellent place to begin a study of Louisbourg. The *Dictionary of Canadian Biography*, Volumes 2, 3 and 4 (also available in French) offers profiles of many of the town's key personalities. The *Historical Atlas of Canada: From the Beginning to 1800*, Plate 24, provides an overview of life in Louisbourg within the North American context. Prepared by Louisbourg historian Kenneth Donovan, the plate examines Louisbourg's fisheries, fortifications, trade patterns, social composition and architecture.

Kenneth Donovan is also the editor of *Cape Breton at 200: Historical Essays in Honour of the Island's Bicentennial* and *The Island: New Perspectives on Cape Breton History, 1713-1990*. Both explore selected themes in Louisbourg's history.

Louisbourg staff historian A.J.B. Johnston is another commentator on Louisbourg's social and administrative institutions. *Religion in Life at Louisbourg, 1713-1758* examines the spiritual life of the townspeople. *The Summer of 1744: A Portrait of Life in 18th-century Louisbourg* is a time capsule of Louisbourg just before the first siege. Both books are available in French as well as English.

Aspects of Louisbourg: Essays on the History of an Eighteenth-century French Community in North America was published to commemorate the 275th anniversary of the founding of Louisbourg. Edited by Eric Krause, Carol

Corbin and William O'Shea, it features essays on the cod fishery, urban development, fortifications, conservation issues and a host of related themes.

One of the liveliest and most informative books on the people of Louisbourg is Christopher Moore's *Louisbourg Portraits: Life in an Eighteenth-century Garrison*. Readers experience Louisbourg through the eyes of five 18th-century townspeople. The work is also available in French.

Readers interested in Louisbourg's reconstruction should consult Terry MacLean's *Louisbourg Heritage: From Ruins to Reconstruction*, a detailed eye-witness account of the exciting years of reconstruction. Anyone with an interest in gastronomy will enjoy *From the Hearth: Recipes from the World of 18th-century Louisbourg*, written by Hope Dunton.

Two CD-ROMs also explore the town's history. *Fortress of Louisbourg*, produced by Fitzgerald Studio, is an encyclopaedia of life in the town. Folkus Atlantic's *Time Travel to the 18th Century* portrays facets of 18th-century life through the media of film and photographs, the majority of which were taken at the Fortress of Louisbourg.

Serious researchers are welcome, with prior arrangement, to view the extensive collection at the Fortress of Louisbourg Library. In addition to general and specialized books on 18th-century life, the collection includes a series of in-house reports prepared by staff historians and archaeologists. A vast print collection details 18th-century costumes, social habits and food. Original documents can be viewed on microfiche.

Researchers may also wish to consult articles in the *Nova Scotia Historical Review*, *Beaver*, *Material History Bulletin*, *Acadiensis*, *Canadian Collector*, *Queen's Quarterly*, *Dalhousie Review* and *American Neptune*. Further information on the Fortress and surrounding areas can be found on the Louisbourg Institute's website: http://fortress.cbu.ca